Dr Janina Scarlet is a licensed clinical psychologist, an award-winning author and a full-time geek. A Ukrainian-born refugee, she survived Chernobyl radiation and persecution. She immigrated to the United States at the age of 12 with her family and later, inspired by the X-Men, developed Superhero Therapy to help patients with anxiety, depression and PTSD. Dr Scarlet is the recipient of the Eleanor Roosevelt Human Rights Award by the United Nations Association for her work on Superhero Therapy. Her work has been featured on *Yahoo!*, the BBC, NPR, *Sunday Times*, CNN, CW, ABC, *The New York Times*, *Forbes* and many other outlets. She regularly consults on books and television shows, including HBO's *The Young Justice*. She was also portrayed as a comic book character in Gail Simone's *Seven Days* graphic novel. Dr Scarlet is the Lead Trauma Specialist at the Trauma and PTSD Healing Center and the Lead Creativity Coach at Creative Community in San Diego, California.

Also by Janina Scarlet

Superhero Therapy
Therapy Quest
Dark Agents
Harry Potter Therapy
Super-Women
Super Survivors
It Shouldn't Be This Way

Unseen, Unheard and Undervalued

Managing Loneliness, Loss of Connection and Not Fitting In

Janina Scarlet, Ph.D.

ROBINSON

ROBINSON

First published in Great Britain in 2023 by Robinson

1 3 5 7 9 10 8 6 4 2

A CIP catalogue record for this book
is available from the British Library.

ISBN: 978-1-47214-769-1

Typeset in Gentium by Initial Typesetting Services, Edinburgh
Printed and bound in Great Britain by Clays Ltd, Elcograf S.p.A.

Papers used by Robinson are from well-managed forests
and other responsible sources.

Robinson
An imprint of
Little, Brown Book Group
Carmelite House
50 Victoria Embankment
London EC4Y 0DZ

An Hachette UK Company
www.hachette.co.uk

www.littlebrown.co.uk

To anyone who'd ever felt lonely in a crowd
or misunderstood by the people closest to them –
I see you. You matter.
And you belong in this world.
Thank you for being wonderful.

Contents

PART 3:
Unheard

PART 4:
Undervalued

PART 5:
Forming a Connection with Yourself

Contents

PART 6 :

Connection with Others

PART 7:
The Impact You Make

Introduction

I closed my book, having reread it so many times that I could recite it without opening it. I slid into my red and white slippers and walked into my older brother's room. He was fifteen years old, and nine years older than me.

'Check,' he said to his best friend and moved his white chess piece across the board. Then he got up and dragged me out of his room.

'Stay out,' he said and slammed the door.

I swallowed.

This was a familiar feeling. *No one wants me around.*

I went into the kitchen to find my mom washing dishes, 'Mom, can we do something together?'

My mom sighed. 'I'm busy. Go to your room and play.'

'But I'm lonely,' I protested.

My mom sighed again and turned off the faucet. 'Come with me.'

I followed her to the living room. She scanned our bookshelves and then pulled out a poem by the notorious Russian poet Korney Chukovsky.

The poem read:

> *Poor Fedotka, the orphan:*
> *Poor Fedotka, he cries,*

1

He doesn't have anyone
Who would soothe and comfort him,
He only has his mom, and his uncle, and his aunt
And his dad, and his grandpa and his grandma.

She read it to me. Then I read it to myself several times, trying to make sense of it.

'What does it mean?' I finally asked her.

My mom laughed. 'Don't you see? Fedotka thought he was lonely. Just like you. Silly boy. He felt like he was an orphan. He completely forgot that he had his whole family.'

She left the poem with me and walked out of the room.

I didn't know the right way to feel but I was pretty sure that whatever I was feeling was wrong. I knew that my mother's intention was to cheer me up, but after reading that poem I felt even worse.

As I was trying to fall asleep that night, I kept thinking about Fedotka, and the more I thought about him, the more I felt like crying, until I felt hot tears run down my face. *The poor boy. He must have felt so lonely.*

In the place between awake and asleep I imagined him into being. He sat beside me, and I held his little hand while he cried. He told me how, even though he had his family, and he wasn't actually orphaned, sometimes he felt as though he was.

'I understand. I feel that way too sometimes,' I said to him.

He gave me a sad smile and nodded.

We cried together and somehow, I felt better. Not because I, as the poem suggested, had to be reminded that I had a family, but because this boy, real or imagined, felt just as lonely as I did. And that meant I was not alone in my loneliness.

The truth is everyone feels lonely. No one is spared from this emotion. Children feel lonely, as do teens and adults. People in relationships feel lonely, as do widowed people, divorced people and single people. Individuals in every profession feel lonely – scientists, lawyers, doctors, CEOs, movie stars, salespeople, waiters, grocery clerks, college students – everyone. And in that, we are all united.

As a licensed clinical psychologist and a trauma specialist, I use stories to help people heal from emotional pain and suffering caused by trauma, abuse and rejection, as well as war, assault, neglect and other traumatic experiences. And what I've come to learn is that even though loneliness is a universal emotion, one we all experience at one point or another, we have also been made to feel ashamed, oppressed and stigmatised about experiencing it.

If you're like me, you might sometimes feel like you're shouting into the void for someone to just see you and to acknowledge that you exist, that you have value, that you are loved.

And perhaps you've felt like the void itself took a vacation and turned its back on you.

That feeling – like no one can really see who you are, like no one *really gets it,* that's loneliness.

Loneliness is often accompanied by feelings of emptiness, depression, anxiety, lethargy, boredom, frustration, irritability and anger. In addition, loneliness is also accompanied by certain unhelpful beliefs. These beliefs include thoughts that if you were to express who you are or how you truly feel, you'd be laughed at, criticised or shamed. Loneliness perpetuates the belief that you're an outsider who's 'just faking it', and that deep inside you don't actually belong – sooner or later, you'll be discovered, kicked out, and then nobody will ever love you.

All of these beliefs are false, created by our mind as an innocent attempt at self-protection – to keep us vigilant at identifying any potential sign of social rejection so we can avoid it in the first place. While our mind's intentions are good (much as I'm sure my mother's intentions were), these false beliefs can make us feel worse and even more alone.

In my case, I've spent most of my life feeling lonely but not fully understanding what loneliness was. I was ashamed of feeling lonely, which lead to me feeling depressed. In an effort to solve this problem, I denied my loneliness and plunged myself into work – any work really, just to keep feelings of loneliness out of my heart.

I went to school early to help the teachers. I volunteered to stay after school to tutor my classmates. I signed up for anything and everything, just to feel useful. *So long as I'm useful, I'm not worthless,* I told myself. *And so long as I'm not worthless, I won't be cast out.*

And yet, the more I ran from loneliness, the lonelier I actually felt. That is, until the tidal wave of loneliness pulled me deep down and forced me to look into its soul.

Into *my* soul.

Once I realised the futility of trying to outrun loneliness, I decided to do the opposite. I stopped running. I dove into it. I studied it. I spent years devouring books and analysing research studies on the topic of loneliness. I reflected on the impact of loneliness on my own life, on the lives of my loved ones, and on the lives of my clients.

I discovered that human beings need more than access to food, sleep and water to survive. We also need to feel a sense of belonging. We need to feel understood and supported. We need to know that our deepest wounds aren't our own unique burdens to carry but are a part of the universal experience.

The more I wrote and spoke publicly about loneliness, the more invitations for training poured in, and I began to comprehend the magnitude of this universal problem. People all over the world, from every culture and background, benefit from learning more about what loneliness is and how to manage it.

That is why I wrote this book. My goal is to reduce the stigma surrounding loneliness, to share some of the most important findings about how to manage it, and to help people foster a sense of belonging. I wrote it to offer some guidance as to how we can lead healthier and more fulfilling lives. My intention is to help you identify how loneliness may show up in your own life, understand how it impacts you, and to help you discover some actionable steps you can take in order to feel seen, heard and valued.

You deserve nothing less.

And I'll be with you every step of the way.

Throughout the pages of this book, I will be your virtual friend. Imagine me as a sidekick to sit in the dark with you, to hold your hand, to help you feel less alone – just as Fedotka did for me.

In order to help you understand your experiences with loneliness, I would like to invite you to fill out the UCLA Loneliness Scale. This questionnaire can help you to identify your specific experiences with loneliness, to be aware when they are occurring, and to determine when you need support.

Please use a pen and paper or an electronic device, such as a computer or your mobile phone, to record and count your answers. Later, you will be invited to fill it out again at the end of the book to see what, if anything, has changed, and if there is anything you might need additional help with.

UCLA Loneliness Scale (Version 3)[1]

Directions: Indicate how often you feel the way described in each of the following statements. Circle one number for each.

Statement	Never	Rarely	Some-times	Always
1. How often do you feel that you are 'in tune' with the people around you?*	1	2	3	4
2. How often do you feel that you lack companionship?	1	2	3	4
3. How often do you feel that there is no one you can turn to?	1	2	3	4

---

1 Russell (1996). Scale is used with permission

	1	2	3	4
4. How often do you feel alone?	1	2	3	4
5. How often do you feel part of a group of friends?*	1	2	3	4
6. How often do you feel that you have a lot in common with the people around you?*	1	2	3	4
7. How often do you feel that you are no longer close to anyone?	1	2	3	4
8. How often do you feel that your interests and ideas are not shared by those around you?	1	2	3	4
9. How often do you feel outgoing and friendly?*	1	2	3	4
10. How often do you feel close to people?*	1	2	3	4
11. How often do you feel left out?	1	2	3	4
12. How often do you feel that your relationships with others are not meaningful?	1	2	3	4
13. How often do you feel that no one really knows you well?	1	2	3	4
14. How often do you feel isolated from others?	1	2	3	4

15. How often do you feel that you can find companionship when you want it?*	1	2	3	4
16. How often do you feel that there are people who really understand you?*	1	2	3	4
17. How often do you feel shy?	1	2	3	4
18. How often do you feel that people are around you but not with you?	1	2	3	4
19. How often do you feel that there are people you can talk to?*	1	2	3	4
20. How often do you feel that there are people you can turn to?*	1	2	3	4

*Items for questions number 1, 5, 6, 9, 10, 15, 16, 19 and 20 should be reversed before scoring them, meaning that you should score 1 as 4, 2 as 3, 3 as 2 and 4 as 1.

NOTE: Your score is the sum of all items.

What score did you get? The scores range from 20–80. Higher scores indicate higher levels of loneliness. This might mean that your needs for belonging are not being met in some capacity. Take a look at the statements in which you scored the highest marks, indicating that this is usually a struggle for you. What are the situations where these challenges come up? For example, you might feel 'shy' when you are around invalidating people who do not allow you to express yourself.

What would have to change (if anything) for your needs to be met? There are neither right nor wrong ways to answer this question but perhaps we can focus on the kindest, most authentic and most compassionate ways to think about this. For example, if you're focusing on #11 on the survey, 'How often do you feel left out?', and if you've answered that you *always* feel left out, what would have to change for you to feel included? Perhaps it is that people would need to be more thoughtful to invite you to events or to check in with you about your preferences or opinions for you to feel more included?

Take some time to consider what your needs are and, if you're willing, write them down so that you can refer back to them later. At the end of the book, you will be invited to take the same survey again. See if anything has changed and what your needs are at that point. Whether your scores change, stay the same, get better or get worse, this is NOT an indication of your personal failure in any way. These questions merely reflect some possible needs you might have that might not currently be met.

How to Get the Most Out of This Book

This book is intentionally broken up into small chapters. As you're reading, take as many breaks as you need to and don't push yourself. Some people like to read quickly, whereas others like to read slowly, take notes and reflect. Some people struggle with brain fog, concentration, motivation, chronic pain or other difficulties. Whatever you are facing, please take care of yourself and your needs as best you can. Feel free to go at it one chapter at a time, or skip around, or reread sections as many times as you need to. Please know that there is no rush, and no 'right' way to read this book.

Some people benefit from having a journal (a notebook or an electronic journal) to write and reflect on their thoughts and experiences as they are reading. Others like to take time to silently reflect. See what works best for you.

You might not relate to everything in this book. That is perfectly okay. Please use what applies to you and feel free to toss out what doesn't. Make this experience your own.

There might be sections that bring up something painful for you. If tears come, let them come. See if you can observe your emotions with curiosity. Perhaps you can ask yourself, *What emotions am I feeling right now? What thoughts or memories is this bringing up for me? Can I be kind to myself as I'm reading this?*

Through the pages of this book, I'll be with you every step of the way. Although we may not know each other, I have written these words specifically for you, to tell you that *you matter.*

You are here for a reason.

And you make a wonderful impact in this world.

TAKE AWAYS

- Know that if you feel lonely, you are not alone in feeling that way. I wrote this book specifically because most of my life I've felt the same way.
- Social connection and belonging are just as crucial for our well-being as physical needs like food, water and shelter.
- Throughout this journey, like a character from a favourite story, I will be alongside you and holding your hand from afar.

PART 1:
Am I the Only One?

PART II

Am I the Only One?

Chapter 1
Hurting for a Hug

I was twelve years old when my family and I immigrated to the United States from Ukraine. I was starting seventh grade and apart from being able to say my name, I didn't speak a word of English.

Being an immigrant and coming from a radioactive country (after the Chernobyl radiation accident), I made an easy bullying target. Kids would ask me if I was radioactive or contagious or if I glowed in the dark.

Things weren't much better at home. My parents and older brother were so traumatised by the move and all of our prior experiences that they had no time for me.

As a result, there wasn't a place where I fit in. Not at home, not in school. Nowhere.

I knew that learning English as quickly as possible would give me the best chance to find new friends. So, I dove into comedy television shows – sitcoms. I watched *Full House* and *Family Matters* with closed captions on and with a big, heavy dictionary in my lap. I translated the words I was reading on the screen as quickly as possible to try to understand the content of the programmes.

After a couple of months, I was able to understand a lot of what I was hearing on the shows with minimal translation.

And in addition to learning English, I was also learning about American culture.

I saw that the families in both shows talked to one another, listened to each other, and gave each other hugs. As I watched these shows, I found myself craving hugs as well. At one point, I squeezed Sam, my brown teddy bear, tears forming in my eyes as I realised how touch-starved I was.

Hugging wasn't common in my culture and in my family. The older I got, the fewer hugs I received. The only time I got a hug was when I was injured.

Watching the kids on *Full House* and *Family Matters* hug their parents 'just because' gave me an idea.

I walked up to my mom, who was slicing cucumbers in the kitchen, and put my arms around her.

'What are you doing?' she yelled, throwing my arms off of her. 'Can't you see I'm chopping vegetables? I could have cut you.'

'I'm sorry,' I said, feeling myself blush. 'I just wanted a hug.'

She stared at me for a moment before answering, 'This isn't *Full House*. I'm not an American mom. We don't hug.'

I stormed off into my room and slammed the door. I picked up my giant dictionary and threw it on the ground with all my fury.

It made a loud thud.

I kicked the dictionary for good measure, and it slid under my bed.

Realising that I would be needing the dictionary to do my homework, I dove on the ground to pick it up, hot tears running down my face. Right as I was on the floor, trying to fish it out, my mother burst into the room.

'Are you okay? Did you fall?' She bent down to look at me. 'Did you get hurt?'

I could barely talk between the sobs, so I just pointed to my arm.

'Aww. You poor girl.' My mom hugged me, and my cheeks burned from the lie.

My mother then proceeded to take me to the emergency room to get my arm X-rayed and get my other arm poked with needles for multiple blood tests. I was so ashamed of myself that I didn't make a sound about any of the poking or prodding. I told myself that I deserved it.

We spent six hours in the emergency room. All for one hug.

It was worth it.

I didn't learn until well into my adulthood that meaningful connection, such as a kind embrace, is a basic human need. We all need to feel seen, heard and valued in order to thrive as human beings.

You might have heard these terms thrown around – seen, heard and valued – but what do they really mean?

Being **Seen** means that someone notices you. They realise when you are not your usual self. They notice your absence and include you in their plans and conversations. For example, when a co-worker thanks you for doing something nice for them or your manager recognises how hard you work, you might feel seen.

17

Being **Heard** means to be heard without interruption, gaslighting or invalidation, but rather with compassion and understanding. It means that the other person is listening to what you have to say, even if they disagree. It means that they try to understand your perspective without criticising you, giving advice or putting you down. For example, if you and your friend have a disagreement but are both able to respectfully hear each other out and validate each other's feelings, you might feel heard.

Being **Valued** means being respected and treated with compassion and kindness, whether it means being given a loving hug or words of support and encouragement. In the workplace, it means that you aren't criticised for making mistakes but are given the help and the support you need and are encouraged to try again. In relationships, it means that your friends, partner or family members do not shame you, put you down or criticise you. It means that they express appreciation or gratitude for you or your actions and speak to you in a gentle and kind tone.

These needs – to be seen, heard and valued – are not egotistic. They are basic human needs. When we are seen, heard and valued, we feel safer and less hypervigilant. We feel emotionally secure and are able to self-soothe when in distress.

When all three of these needs are met – when we feel **seen**, **heard** and **valued** – we experience a sense of **belonging**.

Belonging refers to the feeling that you are a valued part of a group. It means that you matter to a specific person, a pet, a family or a community.

Belonging gives us a sense of emotional safety. Emotional

safety means that you can trust that the people (or animals) in your support system will unconditionally accept you. It means that you do not have to worry about abandonment, rejection, abuse or criticism from your support system.

When these needs are not met from the people we care most about, we feel lonely. Loneliness does not mean being physically alone in a particular space. Rather, loneliness means feeling alone in your heart. It is a kind of soul wound, a feeling like you do not belong. Like you do not matter.

And nothing could be further from the truth. Because you do – you belong and you matter, and you deserve to know and to *feel* like you belong, even if you've been made to feel otherwise in the past.

When we don't have emotional safety, our body goes into high overwhelm, triggering the fight-flight-freeze-or-fawn response. The fight-flight-freeze-or-fawn response is a form of nervous system reaction, in which the body goes into high-alert mode. Rather than focusing on rational decisions, the body will do whatever is necessary to help you survive by fighting for your life, running away, freezing or fawning over someone (people-pleasing) in order to reduce the threat[1] of being hurt or abandoned.

When we lack emotional safety, we might be highly triggered in situations that other people might find safe, or even enjoyable, such as at concerts, amusement parks or restaurants. The lack of emotional safety can create a spike in our

1 Walker (2013)

nervous system even if we are physically safe. In these situations, we can't feel calm because our nervous system is either in active crisis or getting ready for one. For example, a person who had experienced many years of emotional abuse, yelling and invalidation might experience a panic attack – a kind of a flight-and-freeze response – at a football game, even if the people around them are shouting from joy.

For this reason, we are going to learn about how and why belonging is a valid need; one that is critical for your survival. We will learn about different patterns that can cause you to feel emotionally unsafe, so that you can recognise them and learn how to support yourself. In future parts of the book, we will also learn about boundary setting and self-advocacy skills to ensure that your needs are met and addressed as much as possible.

You matter and I care about you, and we will get through this together.

Chapter 2
Together in a Lonely World

In preparing to write this book, I surveyed over three hundred people about their experiences of loneliness in order to better understand what made them feel lonely.

Here are the results of the list I compiled based on the participants' self-reported responses:

LONELY EXPERIENCES:		
Childhood sexual abuse	Overstimulation	Body sensations - dizziness, nausea, brain fog
Abandonment	Migraines	Discomfort with small talk
Emotional abuse	Ghosting	Struggling with intrusive thoughts
Chronic illness and chronic pain	Divorce	Friend break-up
Life-threatening allergies	Chronic thoughts about suicide	Feeling alone in public situations (cafeteria, meetings, parties)
Imposter syndrome	Getting passed up for promotion at work	Harassment

Moving or immigration	Struggling with finances	Surviving a violent situation, like abuse, war or torture
Miscarriage	Incarceration	Feeling invalidated and gaslighted
Experiencing narcissistic abuse	Neglect	Feeling abandoned by the medical system
Eating disorders and body dysmorphia	Fears of being perceived as 'weird' or 'awkward'	Losing someone to suicide
Rejection about one's sexual orientation or gender identity	Social anxiety	Suicide attempt
Bullying	Struggling with dating or finding a partner	Retirement or leaving the military
Ambiguous grief	Addiction	Back-up partners because of fears of abandonment
Loss of a child	Loss of a pet	Loss of a spouse
Panic attacks	Anxiety	Having many friendship circles to have back-up friends
Parentification	Always trying to fit in, but feeling like an outsider	Feeling like you missed out on your childhood

How many of these do you relate to? Sometimes, seeing a mirror representation of our experience of loneliness in another person in real life, on social media, or even in fiction, can actually create a feeling of belonging.

For me, reading the *Harry Potter* books and learning about Harry's experiences of growing up with his relatives and hating summers that he spent with them made me feel seen. Like Harry, I too hated summers because of how lonely I felt. I took classes to advance my studies for three summers in a row when I was a teenager, just to have a reason to leave the house and do something structured with other people my age.

As I mentioned in the previous section, loneliness can be broken up into three subtypes of emotional disconnection: feeling **unseen**, feeling **unheard** and feeling **undervalued**. The first of these, the feeling of being **unseen**, usually feels like a sadness, helplessness and a rejection. On the other hand, feeling **unheard** is often accompanied by feelings of frustration, anger and confusion, where we might doubt our own experiences. Finally, the feeling of being **undervalued** (or 'devalued') refers to feeling like an outcast, an imposter, fearing not being good enough and not fitting in. The latter subtype of loneliness is often accompanied by feelings of anxiety, embarrassment and shame. In upcoming sections, we will delve deeper into each of these and then discuss how we can manage each type of loneliness.

We all have painful experiences we've survived. We all have gone through something we might be ashamed of or too embarrassed to bring up. But the truth is, the more we talk about it, the more we can see that we are not that different. That we all share similar stories with slight differences in minor details.

Underneath it all, we are the same.

Chapter 3
Loneliness Hurts. Literally

When you're feeling sad, have you noticed that you also physically feel the sadness in your body? Your chest might ache, or your stomach might churn, or you might feel short of breath. For me, I feel a tightness in my chest, an overwhelming sense of emptiness in my stomach, and a lump in my throat, as if I'm stifling a sob.

This phenomenon has been well researched. People who experience chronic loneliness often also report physical pain, including headaches, stomach aches and chest pains. Loneliness and physical pain activate our brains in the exact same way, meaning that our brain interprets the emotional pain of loneliness and social exclusion as just as painful – and in many cases, even *more* painful – than physical pain. In fact, when people who are struggling with loneliness take painkillers, such as acetaminophen/paracetamol, their loneliness pain reduces as well.[1]

This research finding does NOT mean that we can solve the global loneliness crisis with pain medication. But it does mean several other things.

First, it means that the pain of loneliness is as real as physical pain, such as migraine pain, stomach aches and back pain.

1 DeWall, et al. (2010); Eisenberger (2012)

In some instances, loneliness can also exacerbate physical pain by activating the pain neural receptors in our brains.

Second, it means that people who struggle with addiction to prescription medication, especially opiate medications, as well as people who struggle with addiction to illicit drugs and alcohol, might very likely be using these substances to cope with excruciating loneliness.

Third, and most important, it means that the solution to healing this type of pain must include cultivating a deep sense of belonging.

Among the many health benefits of belonging, including improved physical health, improved mood, reduced physical and mental health symptoms, belonging also boosts the release of endorphins and oxytocin hormones.[2] Endorphins are a part of our internal pain-regulating chemicals called *endogenous opioids*. These internally produced opioids help us regulate not only our physical pain, but also our emotional pain. This means that rather than relying on (and getting addicted to) opiate medications, which tend to facilitate worsened pain once they wear off, we can foster the release of our own internal pain-killing chemicals by giving or receiving support to others and cultivating our sense of belonging.

Here's an experiment that shows how this technique works. Researchers at the University of Wisconsin tested how giving and receiving emotional support impacts physical pain levels. In their experiment, the researchers invited sixteen married

2 Chu (2017); Xu & Roberts (2010)

couples into the lab. All partners were asked to fill out a questionnaire measuring their satisfaction in their marriage. For each couple, one of the partners was placed into an MRI and was told that they would receive mild electric shocks on either the left or the right ankle. One third of the participants underwent this process alone. Another third of the participants had a stranger (the experimenter) hold their hand during this process. The remainder of the participants had their spouse hold their hand.

Even though all the participants in the study received the same level of shock, those who had someone holding their hand (whether it was the experimenter or the participant's spouse) exhibited a lower activation in the pain centres of their brain. Interestingly, the people whose spouses held their hand during the procedure reported significantly less distress in response to the shocks compared to the stranger holding their hand, as well as the condition in which no one held their hand. And the better the quality of the marriage (as reported in the questionnaires), the less the participants' pain centres were activated in response to the shock.[3]

Just like for the participants in this study, social support is vital to your physical and emotional health. So, if you are struggling with excruciating physical and/or emotional pain right now, if your loneliness feels like it is swallowing you faster than quicksand, please know that there is a reason for that – you are not meant to face this kind of pain alone.

3 Coan, et al. (2006)

The lack of social support and belonging is so hurtful that humans and animals alike suffer when they are isolated. In fact, because mammals are social creatures, loneliness can cause so much distress that they can act out their internal pain by using self-harm. Monkeys, cats and dogs self-harm when they are kept in social isolation without contact with other mammals. Some scratch out patches of their fur from distress and others stop eating and fail to thrive, all due to loneliness. Thankfully, the effects of self-harm and failure to thrive can often be reversed when the isolated mammals are socialised again and are given affection from others.[4] This means that the pain of being isolated, physically or emotionally, causes such severe pain that sometimes we don't know a healthy way to manage the magnitude of it.

I'll be honest, I cried as I wrote this section. My heart still aches for everyone who's ever self-harmed because of the excruciating feelings of loneliness, whether they are humans, cats, dogs or monkeys. A famous study by Harry Harlow in the late 1950s shows that when monkeys are raised in isolation, they cling on to anything that resembles a caring parental touch, even a dirty cloth diaper. Whenever the researchers tried changing the cloth diaper for sanitary reasons, the monkeys became aggressive and fought the researchers, while also exhibiting high levels of distress.

Harry Harlow then conducted a new experiment. He began studying the baby monkeys' interactions with two fake

4 Reinhardt & Rossell (2001)

surrogate mothers – one wire monkey that fed them with a bottle and one soft cloth-covered monkey that did not provide food. Harlow discovered that outside of feeding time, the baby monkeys spent approximately 85 per cent of their time cuddling with the cloth mother.[5]

And if you are tearing up right now, wishing that you could just cradle and soothe those poor baby monkeys and give them all the love they clearly deserved and needed, I feel your pain.

I am mortified to read about this study and to write about it. And at the same time, the results of this study clearly show us that mammals who are starving from loneliness and lack of touch are in high distress. And if our hearts can break for the baby monkeys who self-harm because they are lonely, and who fight for a used diaper the same way a small child fights for their teddy bear, then perhaps we can look at human beings with the same loving eyes. And if there is a lonely inner child inside each of us, then we can perhaps cuddle and comfort that inner child the same way we might feel the pull to comfort the tiny monkeys who just want to be held.

Try it out. Place your hands on your heart centre to give yourself a small hug. Or perhaps wrap yourself in a warm blanket and snuggle a pillow or a teddy bear. You might feel silly at first, but I encourage you to try anyway, if you are willing. If you are not willing, or if this doesn't feel good or safe to do, please feel free to disregard and ignore this exercise. Listen to your body. Do what feels right and safe to you.

5 Harlow (1959)

Because it doesn't matter if you're nine, thirty-nine or eighty-nine. We all need and deserve to be soothed, held and supported. And when we receive it, either from ourselves or from other people, our bodies release oxytocin.

Oxytocin is a hormone involved in bonding and soothing (self-soothing and soothing of others).[6] It is also a natural anti-inflammatory, and it appears to strengthen our nervous system, our cardiovascular health and our immune system,[7] as well as causing a deceleration of ageing, and a longer lifespan.[8] In simpler terms, oxytocin is *really* good for you.

So, if you need a hug, give yourself one. You deserve a hug whenever you need it.

And I'm sending you a virtual one from afar.

6 Crespi (2016)
7 Carter, et al. (2020)
8 Epel (2020); Epel & Lithgow (2014); Xu & Roberts (2010)

Chapter 4
'Loneliness is the New Smoking'

Loneliness hurts because it's supposed to. It hurts because this is how our brain tells us that we have a need; a starvation for belonging.

For a long time, scientists have known that social connectedness is important for people's psychological well-being. However, only recently are we starting to understand how critical it is to our survival. According to the US Surgeon General, Dr Vivek Murthy, loneliness has become a silent epidemic, posing as one of the top reasons for emergency room visits and medical appointments. In the US and the UK, approximately 20 per cent of emergency room visits are related to loneliness, where the presenting symptoms include panic attacks, dizziness, severe emotional distress and heightened physical pain.[1]

Loneliness doesn't just affect how you feel; it affects how healthy you are, and how long you live. The longest-running study analysing the factors that lead to happiness was conducted at Harvard University. The researchers at Harvard found that meaningful social connections are good for our health and can even help to prevent Alzheimer's Disease. On the other hand, this study found that unhappy relationships in which

1 Murthy (2020)

partners spent a lot of time arguing, and in which one partner felt unseen and undervalued by the other, were worse for the participants' health than getting a divorce. Finally, this study found that while loneliness can lead to a shorter lifespan, having meaningful social relationships can actually extend our lives.[2]

Some researchers have now dubbed loneliness as 'The New Smoking'[3] due to the fact that loneliness is as dangerous to our health as smoking fifteen cigarettes per day or daily alcohol abuse. This does not mean that loneliness affects our lungs the way smoking does, nor does it mean that it affects our liver the same way alcohol does. What it does mean is that loneliness can shorten our lifespan the same way as chronic drinking and smoking. Specifically, chronic loneliness has been linked to increased risk of heart disease; Alzheimer's Disease; increased mental health pathology, including depression, anxiety, assumptions of worthlessness and burdensomeness; as well as inflammation, immune and autoimmune problems, higher risk of suicide and higher risk of premature mortality.[4]

Furthermore, the majority of suicide risk factors outlined by the Centers for Disease Control, National Library of Medicine, the Mayo Clinic and the Trevor Project, such as going through a recent loss or a break-up, lack of social support, going through trauma, anxiety, depression, insomnia, substance abuse, bullying or prejudice, and struggling with sexual orientation or gender identity, can all be tied to loneliness. On the other hand,

2 Waldinger (2015)
3 Holt-Lunstad, et al. (2015); Tate (2018)
4 Cacioppo, et al. (2009); Friedmann, et al. (2006)

the top suicide-prevention factors are all tied to creating a sense of community and belonging. These factors include access to culturally competent care, creating safe and caring communities, positive connections with others, as well as family support and acceptance.

This means that the need for social connection is not a reflection of 'neediness', nor is it a personal weakness. It is our path to survival.

In his groundbreaking research paper on the theory of human motivation, American psychologist Abraham Maslow created the hierarchy of basic human needs, which are as follows:

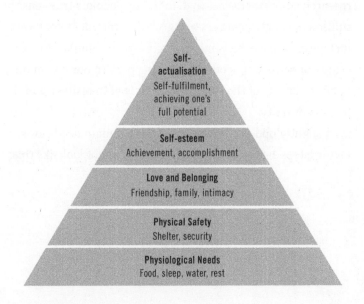

1. Physiological needs (food, sleep, water, rest)
2. Physical safety (shelter, security)

3. Love and belonging (friendship, family, intimacy)
4. Self-esteem (achievement, accomplishment)
5. Self-actualisation (self-fulfilment, achieving one's full potential)

Maslow's model is very well thought out and, for the most part, it still holds true today. But over the past few decades, scientists have discovered some of its flaws. The main differences between Maslow's original model and what scientists have discovered is that love and belonging are as vital to our survival as food, sleep and water. Another difference is that newer research points to the fact that, for many people, a true sense of fulfilment comes from personal growth, which does not have to include external achievement or self-esteem. Similarly, discovering our sense of purpose and giving back to our community seems to be one of the top factors that lead to resilience in the face of adversity.[5]

A slightly updated hierarchy of basic human needs for surviving (steps 1–3) and thriving (steps 4–5) might look like this:

5 Hamby, et al. (2020)

The Surviving and Thriving Hierarchy:

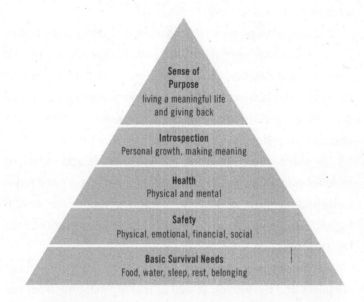

1. Basic survival needs (food, water, sleep, rest, **belonging**)
2. Safety (physical, **emotional,** financial, **social)**
3. Physical and mental health
4. Introspection, meaning making and personal growth
5. Sense of purpose and giving back

The first step includes the same basic needs Maslow identified in his original model – food, water, sleep and rest – but it also includes a sense of belonging. This could mean having a supportive partner or friend, having a pet to care for, or a supportive community, for example. A sense of belonging doesn't just make us feel better emotionally, it can give us the will to

35

live in the most challenging of circumstances and can allow us a better chance of survival.[6]

The second step shows the importance of safety and its many facets. Safety can be physical (such as a shelter and protection from physical violence, abuse or war), emotional (such as receiving emotional support and/or being able to manage emotional distress), financial (knowing that you are able to afford your basic needs) and social (knowing that you won't be cast out).

The third step in meeting our basic needs and surviving includes our physical and mental health. When we are physically and mentally healthy, we are able to reduce our mental fog and our mental blocks in order to thrive and advance to the last two steps.

The fourth step includes introspection (learning about ourselves and the world), as well as making meaning from our experiences, both the good and the painful ones.

Finally, step five includes finding our sense of purpose and giving back to our community, so that we are able to thrive even after the most horrific experiences.[7] This does not mean that we silver-line our traumas, nor does it mean that we will never get knocked off course. Our painful experiences hurt, and they affect us just as they would affect anyone else. And if we can surround ourselves with people who care and offer love and support for others in similar situations, then we will likely feel less alone in the process.

6 Friedmann, et al. (2006); Xu & Roberts (2010)
7 Frankl (1985)

Our life is forever changing. Sometimes, we will cycle through steps one to five, and at other times, we will fall back to step two, for example. In these cases, we will need to give ourselves the compassion and the understanding that we require to work through the stages again. Wherever you are today, you are doing your best and you deserve the love, support and gentleness that you need to meet yourself there.

I see how hard you are working. I know it's hard. And I'm with you every step of the way.

Chapter 5
Stress and Loneliness

For the longest time, scientists have believed that stress wreaks havoc on our health. And while that's partially true, it seems that the overall picture is actually more complicated.

Let's start by defining stress. Stress is a response to a stressor, such as a work deadline or receiving a parking ticket.

There are two types of stress – adaptive (also known as *hormetic stress*) and toxic stress. Scientists are now finding that it is the toxic stress that negatively impacts our health, not the adaptive stress.

But what is the difference between the two?

Some of the main differences between toxic stress and adaptive stress are how important the specific situation is to us and how much support we have going through it. Support, in this case, refers to both social support and self-support (also known as self-care).

Toxic stress can look like receiving harsh criticism from your boss, or pressure from your partner to earn more money, or your own internal self-critic telling you that you are failing at life. Toxic stress can also include taunting or bullying from your group members or your competitors while you are working on an important project.

On the other hand, an example of adaptive stress is

preparing for a tournament you are really excited to be a part of while your friends, family members and other supporters are cheering you on. It can also be working on a cause with others who share your ideals and support you in this process. Sure, preparing for a tournament or working on an important cause can be stressful, and even exhausting, but if you are working on something you believe in and have a good support system, you will thrive.

Toxic stress typically involves a stressor (such as a tight deadline at work or undergoing an illness) and a toxic environment, in which you are made to feel small and degraded. Therefore, the definition of toxic stress includes not only the stressor itself but also adversity such as abuse, neglect and feeling devalued and invalidated. Because of this, toxic stress can make us feel physically and emotionally unsafe, physically sick, and speed up our ageing process.[1]

The toxic environment could be one in which the stressor is occurring (for example, being bullied in school or at work), or environments in which the stressor is being processed (for example, telling your family members about being bullied only to have them invalidate you or make fun of you for it). As a result, we are likely to feel unheard and devalued, leading us to feel alone in this experience.

Therefore, we can think about toxic stress through the following formula:

Toxic stress = stressful event(s) + lack of support + loneliness

1 Epel (2020)

In this case, loneliness refers to feeling alone in the stressful experience, with no one to emotionally support you through it, or receiving abuse from others, along with self-neglect and self-criticism.

On the other hand, adaptive stress involves thinking of the stressor as an indication of our core values while having emotional support from others. For example, stress about a work presentation could mean that you really care about your job, which can encourage you to prepare well. If you have an encouraging boss, friend or partner, and are able to take breaks to recharge while preparing for your presentation, you are likely to actually benefit from this type of stress.

Overall, adaptive stress is not only healthy for us, but it also has the complete opposite effects on our physical and mental health compared to toxic stress. Specifically, adaptive stress can make us feel more energised, can boost our immune system, and it might even slow down our ageing process.[2] And meaningful social support, such as a hug from a loved one, can reduce stress hormones in our body and create a more adaptive, healthier response.[3] For more information about adaptive stress, check out *The Upside of Stress* by Kelly McGonigal.[4]

It seems that social support and the permission for self-care are the key factors in determining how our bodies will react to stress. These factors appear to be the difference between the

2 Epel (2020); McGonigal (2016)
3 Berretz, et al. (2022)
4 McGonigal (2016)

toxic effects of stress and the adaptive response that allow us to be healthier and happier.

Stress is an inevitable part of life. And if we have a good support system, if we know that someone is in our corner to bear witness to our pain or cheer us on, then we can get through just about anything.

And if you haven't had this kind of support when you needed it, please know that I see your pain. I know it hurts. And I am with you. I believe in you. We are going to get through this together.

Chapter 6
The Many Faces of Loneliness

Look around you. As you walk on the street in your neighbour-hood, as you walk into a store, as you walk into work or log on for your work meeting or scroll through social media, every face that you see, every voice that you hear – these are the faces of loneliness.

Every single one of these individuals has been lonely at one point of their life. Many of them feel lonely right now, in this very moment. Some perhaps wish they could scream at the top of their lungs, 'Can anyone see me right now? Don't you people realise that I'm suffocating from loneliness?'

But perhaps their voices get drowned out by the ongoing stigma of loneliness, by the heavy lump in their throats, or by the overwhelming terror of being rejected for reaching out for connection.

Loneliness is often misunderstood because it is confused with **social isolation** and **solitude**, but the three experiences are vastly different from one another.

Social isolation has been used as punishment in relation-ships (this is also called punishment by rejection) or in solitary confinement. Solitary confinement is a form of institutional punishment in which a person is temporarily placed in an iso-lated cell with no interaction with other people. A meta-analysis that combined the data across 382,440 inmates found that when people were placed in solitary confinement, they were more likely to self-harm or attempt suicide.[1] Given the research studies in which monkeys and other mammals self-harm when they are isolated from others,[2] the solitary confinement findings are not surprising. Devastating and heartbreaking, but not surprising.

Like solitary confinement, punishment by rejection is also very damaging. Punishment by rejection is seen in some relationships when one person is angry at another and, as a result, intentionally withdraws affection from the other person. This type of affection withdrawal is meant to hurt the other person.

And it does. So much.

Silent treatment (also known as *stonewalling*) is another example of punishment by rejection in some relationships. Silent treatment is different from the *freeze response*, in which the person may want to engage but may feel too intimidated, triggered and overwhelmed to respond. Unlike the freeze response, the silent treatment is intentional and is very harmful to the other individual.

In cases of punishment by rejection, the person who withdraws affection, love, warmth or communication from the other is essentially telling them, 'You no longer exist or matter to me.' This is why some people with a history of traumatic neglect or abandonment feel undervalued and might even consider suicide when they feel rejected by their partner, friend or

1 Luigi et al. (2020)
2 Reinhardt & Rossell (2001)

family member. This feeling of being punished by a rejection of love or affection can sometimes feel worse than dying.

Unlike punishment by rejection, some individuals choose to self-isolate, especially when struggling with depression, trauma, addiction, physical or mental pain, etc. Sometimes, the choice to spend some alone time might be out of self-care and sometimes it might be out of self-punishment. The latter example comes from the belief that others are better off without them, or due to the terror that they will be rejected and abandoned by other people. Although self-isolation is often intended to reduce emotional pain, it can sometimes worsen it.

Unlike social isolation (self-imposed or otherwise), **solitude** is an active decision to spend time alone as a way of practising self-care. Going to a quiet place, like a forest or a meadow, spending time alone at a café or in your room while listening to music, writing a journal, reading or collecting your thoughts to recharge – these are all examples of solitude. Intentionally taking a day or two to read, watch TV shows or play video games in solitude before diving back into a busy environment are also examples of solitude.

Although the actions of self-imposed social isolation and solitude can look similar externally, they vary in internal motivation. Self-imposed isolation is motivated by a desire to avoid feeling any potential pain and discomfort, whereas solitude is motivated by a desire for healing and self-reflection. And because the intentions are different, the outcomes are different too.

While isolation tends to worsen the feelings of loneliness and depression, solitude reduces loneliness and leaves the individual feeling recharged and realigned with their core values.

Keep in mind that unlike isolation and solitude, both of which occur *away* from other people, loneliness can occur *regardless* of whether or not you're in the company of others. In fact, many people feel lonelier when they are around hurtful or invalidating people than when they are physically alone.

When going through trauma or loneliness, social support can be helpful in many ways. Specifically, the support of caring friends and group therapy members can provide the validation and support that we might otherwise not be able to receive, especially from people who harmed us in the past. In addition, people who have meaningful social support at least once per week appear to have no additional risk factors to their lifespan even when undergoing highly stressful events. Finally, people who have meaningful social support on at least a weekly basis appear to demonstrate healthier and longer lifespans.[3]

People of all backgrounds, cultures and walks of life experience loneliness. People might feel lonely after the death of a beloved pet, when they're ill, when they've had a miscarriage or when they are discriminated against for race, religious beliefs, their gender identity or sexual orientation. And if you are feeling lonely right now, please know that whatever you are going through, your pain makes sense. Anyone in your situation would feel the same way you are feeling right now.

3 Coghlan, (2013); Xu & Roberts (2010)

I see your pain. It's real. And, of course, it hurts. I so wish I could take it all away from you. And I know that I can't.

The truth is that our feelings are meant to be felt. That's why they are called *feelings*. The more you suppress your need to express your emotions, the more emotional and physical distress you are likely to endure.

Think of your emotions like a fizzy drink. The more we shake the fizzy drink bottle without opening it to release the pressure, the more likely it is to explode.

But what happens if instead of stifling our feelings and bottling them up, we open them up slowly over time, just like we might be able to do with a shaken bottle of a fizzy drink? If we can be patient, and allow ourselves to mindfully open the bottle, the drink becomes flat and settled.

What's the worst thing that will happen if you open the shaken bottle too quickly? It might explode. But it won't explode for ever. It will settle shortly after, the built-up pressure having been released now. And just like the pressurised fizzy drink, your emotions, including your feelings of loneliness, can soothe and settle over time too.

In the next sections of this book, we will be learning different sets of skills for your mental health toolbox to help you better manage your feelings of loneliness. There are some experiences that many of us share and there are some experiences that may be unique to you. The truth is that only you are the expert in *you* and *your* emotions, and that means that no one can tell you how you should feel. Whatever emotions or reactions you have in any given situation, those feelings are valid and there is a reason why you feel the way that you do. Your emotions are real, and they make sense. Anyone in your specific situation with your specific experiences would feel the same way.

The first of the skills we will be learning is to name your experience. There is a saying, 'Name it and you tame it.'[4] Naming your experiences can allow you to acknowledge what you are going through, so that over time, you can build mindful awareness of your experiences and learn how to respond to them in a kind and loving way.

For example, you might say to yourself, 'I feel lonely right now,' or, 'I feel angry, sad, lonely and irritable.' See if you can name your feelings without any judgement. See if you can observe and study these emotions. Just name them to yourself and observe them with curiosity, as if you're a scientist or a detective, and then make a note of how the naming makes you feel.

4 Neff & Germer (2018)

TAKE AWAYS

- Loneliness can be caused by being unseen, unheard or undervalued.
- The needs to be seen, heard and valued are basic human needs and you deserve to have your needs met.
- Your experiences are valid even if the people in your immediate circle fail to see you, hear you or understand you.
- The more you suppress your needs and emotions, the more emotional and physical distress you are likely to endure.
- Naming your experiences can allow you to acknowledge what you are going through, so that over time, you can build mindful awareness of your experiences and learn how to respond to them in a kind and loving way.

PART 2:
Unseen

Chapter 7
Death and Noodle Soup

'Did you hear?' Lauren said, pulling me aside after our ninth-grade biology class. 'Tom died.'

I was stunned.

I didn't know Tom too well, but we had been in similar school circles for two years at that point. At fourteen years old, this was my first experience of a young person's death.

I don't remember the rest of the school day, as my attention weaved in and out. When I got home, my parents sat around the kitchen table. They quietly slurped on noodle soup and there was a deafening silence between them.

Did they get into a fight again?

'What's the matter?' my mother asked in a flat tone.

My father kept slurping his soup.

I just shook my head.

'You look like someone died,' my mother said in the same flat tone.

My father kept slurping his soup.

'Someone did,' I said, tears now stinging my cheeks on the way down. 'My friend, Tom, died yesterday of a drug overdose. His funeral is on Sunday.'

My mom shrugged. 'What are you going to do? People die.

You crying about it won't bring him back. Now, go wash up and come eat.'

I stared at her, silently pleading, but screaming on the inside for her to see me. But she went back to her food and her gaze abandoned me. I looked to my father, desperate for an ounce of compassion.

But my father kept slurping his soup.

The thing many people can't understand about grief until they've fully experienced it is the deafening sound of silence that only the bereaved can hear, as well as how the bereaved feel both invisible and also the centre of unwanted attention and gossip.

'I was so used to him calling out my name when he was sick, that now I don't know what to do with myself,' one of my clients, 'Carrie'[1], shared with me.

Carrie married her husband, 'Keith', when she graduated nursing school at twenty-five. She had just turned sixty-one when Keith was diagnosed with a terminal illness.

Carrie retired early from her job as a nurse in the ICU to become a full-time carer for Keith. 'Seeing him go from the independent, able-bodied man that I knew to someone who needed round-the-clock support was devastating. It was unreal.'

'People don't understand how lonely it is to be a carer for a family member,' Carrie shared with me at a later time. 'Friends reach out to check on him but forget to check on me. Most days, I forget to eat until I am starving. They invite us out with them,

1 This is not her real name

not realising that his condition doesn't allow him to go out, and I can't leave him at home alone.'

Carrie struggled with pervasive loneliness until she joined a carers' support group.

'I still feel lonely,' she said to me a few months after joining the support group, 'but it's almost like I'm not alone in my loneliness. And that helps.'

When Keith, died, Carrie reported feeling both devastated and relieved.

'He was the love of my life,' she said, showing me a picture of the two of them in front of the Eiffel Tower. 'He was my partner and my best friend. And it almost feels like I lost him twice, first when he got diagnosed, and then again when he died. This is the most excruciating pain I've ever felt. But on some level, I'm also relieved. And I feel so guilty about that. Over the past year that he's been sick, I sometimes wished that he would die peacefully in his sleep. Who does that? I feel so terrible about that.'

'Grief is so confusing,' I told her. 'It's devastating enough to watch the love of your life slowly die in front of your eyes over such an extended period. But there's also so much ambiguity to this limbo period. It's hard to know how to feel.

'Most people who take care of a dying loved one find themselves secretly hoping for it to be over, not because they don't care but specifically because they do. Seeing a loved one suffering is excruciating and most of us would do anything to alleviate their pain. We'd suffer on their behalf if we could. And we do.

'And there's a confusing dichotomy that happens for most of us – we both dread losing our loved one and also wish that their suffering would end. We might also be yearning to be able to grieve – a kind of grief that we might not allow ourselves when a loved one is still alive.'

Carrie nodded. 'It really is confusing. I'm devastated that he's gone. But I'm relieved too. And there are days where I realise that I can take care of myself now, and at the same time, I would give anything to hear him calling my name again. Because on the one hand, he's not suffering any more, and on the other, having a sick husband was better than having no husband at all. And it's true that I'm free now, I don't have anyone to take care of, but I don't even know who I am any more. I've been a nurse most of my life, I've been a carer over the past year, but what do I do now? I'm still trying to sort that part out.'

Carrie also mentioned that perhaps the loneliest part of loss wasn't being home without Keith, it was other people not understanding what she was going through.

'The first few weeks after he died, people called and texted. They brought food and checked on me. And then about a month later, it all just stopped. They all moved on but I'm still grieving. Alone. And what most people don't want to think about is that it will happen to them too. We will all lose some of the people dearest to us. It might be "normal", but we shouldn't normalise this kind of pain.'

Unfortunately, Carrie is not alone in her experience. Most bereaved people receive on average between one and six months of social support from their community. After that, most people either forget or feel ashamed about not having reached out, so they continue not to.

'Even when I am out at dinner with friends now, I feel invisible,' Carrie said. 'They are all coupled, and I feel like an odd person out. They talk about anniversaries, and I won't have any more of those. Most of them ask me how I'm doing but expect me to say that I'm "fine". I'm not fine. Who would be? I wish they wouldn't be afraid to ask me about Keith. About our times together, about my memories with him. I think that people think that if their questions bring tears to my eyes, then they shouldn't ask them. But that's not true. Sharing memories of him and having someone with me when I'm grieving helps me heal.'

Like Carrie, many bereaved individuals struggle with grieving alone. Oftentimes it is because their friends might erroneously think that it is their job to 'cheer up' the bereaved, to 'make them feel better', and not to remind them of their pain. However, for most of us who are struggling with grief, we aren't necessarily looking for a distraction. We are looking for someone with the courage to bear witness to our pain. For someone to hold our hand and create space for us, where we feel safe enough to fall apart.

'The conversations I appreciate the most aren't the ones in which people try to cheer me up or avoid talking about Keith,' Carrie said. 'The ones I appreciate the most are ones where people ask me, "Would you be open to talking about Keith or would you rather be distracted right now?" I appreciate that so much more than people trying to make that choice for me.'

Even the most well-meaning people misstep when caring for a bereaved person.

'I'm so sick of people telling me, "At least he's not suffering any more," or, 'It's for the best," or, "He wouldn't want you to be sad,"' Carrie said. 'I just want to scream at them that they don't know what he would have wanted. Everyone just wants to *fix* this for me. And what I want is for someone to really *see* me, to bear witness to my pain. It doesn't *fix* it, but it sure does help.'

People who are undergoing grief are most likely to feel lonely when they feel unseen and feel most supported when they feel seen and heard. It doesn't seem like much but bearing witness to the suffering of another is more healing than any advice that anyone can give.

People who lost a partner, a child (including miscarriage), people going through a divorce or a job loss, people who lost their pet, all go through excruciating grief, and what makes it most excruciating is loneliness. We can get through just about anything if we have a good support system, a system in which we feel seen, heard and cared for. And when we don't, even the 'smallest' obstacle can seem too much for us to bear. This does not mean we're 'weak' or 'broken'. Rather, it is because in addition to the pain we're carrying, we're also carrying the burden of loneliness.

One of the best books on managing grief I have ever read is *It's Okay That You're Not Okay* by Megan Devine.[2] I highly recommend it.

2 Devine (2017)

If you need support but aren't sure how to ask for it, here are some ways you might be able to meet your needs when you are grieving:

1. **Tell people what you need.** Be direct and clear about your needs. It is perfectly okay for you to say something like, 'I appreciate you trying to cheer me up but what would actually help me is talking about this loss, crying, and just having you listen without interrupting me.'

    No, you are not being demanding; you are being direct. You are advocating for your needs. It's okay to do that. It helps you to get your needs met and it helps others to know how to support you.

2. **Don't be afraid to interrupt.** If someone launches into an unhelpful advice-giving mode or is sharing something unhelpful with you while you are grieving, it is perfectly okay to interrupt this process.

    You're not being rude. You're setting a boundary. For example, you can say, 'I'm going to stop you right there. I know you're trying to help and what would actually be more helpful is if you just listen' (or whatever else you need in that moment, such as 'giving me some space to grieve and process without advice giving').

3. **Feel free to share your needs with your loved ones**, so that they have a guide about how to support you. For example, 'I'm very grateful to all of you for all your support during this difficult time. Many of you have asked what you can do to help. What helps me is when people

reach out by text while giving me a choice as to whether or not I want to reply, such as, "Hi, I'm thinking of you. I would love to chat if you're up for it but no pressure to respond." I also appreciate being able to talk about my loved one and being able to share my feelings and memories without advice or without others trying to cheer me up. I may also pull back from responding for a bit. None of it is personal, it's just me taking time to grieve. Thank you so much for all your support and understanding.'

4. **Remember that it's okay for you to pull away from people** who are critical of your grief process and who aren't following your requests. The grieving process is hard enough. It's a lot harder if you consistently have to defend how you do it.

5. **Join a grief support group** or another support group where you feel seen and heard.

6. **Create a 'cheat sheet' for others.** Most people mean well and still might fail to follow your outlined requests. It doesn't mean they don't care; it likely means they're not skilful in this process. It's perfectly okay to repeat yourself and it's okay to create a 'cheat sheet' for others. On it, you can outline phrases you want to hear and actions you want people to take to make you feel seen and supported. Feel free to give these cheat sheets out and carry some with you.

An example of a grief support cheat sheet:

I know you're trying to help me. Here are some ways I'd like to be supported:

- *Say 'I'm so sorry for your loss.'*
- *Don't ask me to 'move on' or 'accept it'. Instead, ask me to tell you about my loved one. Sharing stories about them helps me heal.*
- *Ask if it's okay to hold my hand or give me a hug. Don't take it personally and please don't force me if I don't want to.*
- *Listen to me talk or watch me cry without interrupting me or trying to stop me from crying and without trying to cheer me up.*
- *Ask me if there are any chores or tasks I need help with. Doing this by myself is hard.*
- *Don't take it personally if I cancel plans or don't respond to you. It's a part of my grieving process.*
- *Say 'Thank you so much for sharing that with me.'*

These steps really do help me with my grieving process. Thank you for supporting me. Feel free to hold on to this card.

Not all of these steps will be possible. Do what you can. Remember, this is your healing journey. You deserve to be seen and supported in the way that you need to be.

Chapter 8
Am I Overreacting?
(No, You are Not)

I had dreamed of moving to California since I was twelve years old. So, when I first got into a university in Los Angeles for my undergraduate programme, I was thrilled.

But less than a month before I was due to move to Los Angeles from New York City, I received a letter notifying me that my financial aid had been denied. This meant that I would not be moving to California, at least not that year.

'What's the big deal?' my mother said. 'Now you can go to school in New York. Stay here and save money. Just be practical.'

You just don't get it, I wanted to argue. *It's not about being practical, it's about my dream.* But I didn't say any of that. Instead, I just said, 'Okay, thanks, Mom,' and walked outside.

I sat on the steps in front of my building and read the letter again. There was no way I would be able to come up with enough money in time to move to California by the start of the school year.

Mascara-stained tears dripped onto the letter and my eyes burned.

'Excuse me, young lady,' I heard a familiar voice speak above me.

When I looked up, I saw our local politician and a bodyguard on either side of him. He campaigned in our neighbourhood often, and I'd met him several times before, even interviewed him for my school paper.

That's so nice, he must have seen me crying and wants to make sure I'm okay, I thought.

'Hi,' I managed to say, and tried my best to wipe my face. Judging by the black streaks of wet mascara on my hands, I realised that I must have looked like a racoon.

'Hi,' the politician said and introduced himself.

'I know who you are, sir,' I said. 'I've interviewed you—'

'Great!' he interrupted and stepped closer to me. His breath smelled of alcohol. 'Well, I'm up for a re-election this fall, and I hope you will vote for me.'

Is he serious? I thought.

But out loud I said, 'I'm not eighteen yet; I'm not old enough to vote.'

'Got it,' he said and moved past me. 'I'll just talk to your parents, then.'

He was about to ring my doorbell.

'We aren't citizens yet,' I said. 'We're immigrants.'

'Got it,' he said with a smile that didn't reach his eyes. He stepped down off our porch and motioned to his bodyguards. 'Let's go.'

He then turned to face me one more time. 'Tell your friends and neighbours to vote for me.' And then he walked away.

I felt insignificant and small in that moment.

Invisible.

And a part of me thought it wasn't a big deal. *After all,* I told myself, *he's an important person who is busy and has no time for my problems.*

But the other part of me was angry. *What a jerk,* I thought. *He could have at least asked me if I was okay. He didn't even care.*

But the first part of me won over. *Stop being a baby,* I silently told myself, *the world doesn't revolve around you.*

When we are unseen, especially in such a blatant way, many of us jump into self-invalidation, again failing to see the core of our own experience. And it is only when someone else can truly see us or when we can truly see ourselves that it can shift.

'Are you okay?' my neighbour asked me a few minutes after my interaction with the politician.

I looked up at him and tried to collect myself. 'I . . . I didn't get the financial aid I needed to attend a university I wanted to go to.'

'Oh, bummer,' he said. He was an older man with a kind smile. And although we lived on the same block, this was the first time we'd spoken.

'I'm so sorry,' he said. 'That's really disappointing. Which university was it?'

And although the total amount of time we'd talked was approximately the same as my conversation with the politician, my neighbour's kindness, his enquiry and his tone made me feel seen and cared for.

And if you are struggling to comprehend a situation where you were unseen, made to feel insignificant and unimportant, please know that you deserve better. You are not exaggerating. You are not being 'dramatic'. You are not 'overreacting'.

One of my clients, 'Danielle', asked me one afternoon, 'Am I invisible?'

It wasn't the first time she spent hours agonising over the best way to write the perfect text message to her friends in their group chat. And it wasn't the first time that only one of her friends responded, having only replied to a small part of her message.

'How does it make you feel?' I asked. 'You spent hours trying to write and rewrite this text to get such an indirect response from only one person.'

'Unseen,' she said, as her voice started to break. 'I just feel invisible, you know?'

She pulled a box of tissues closer to her. 'I just don't understand them. I would never not respond because I know the agony it puts me through. How can someone do that?'

Like Danielle, most of us have *felt* unseen. But what does *unseen* actually mean?

To be unseen means to feel ignored, disregarded or talked over. It means being unnoticed when you are crying or in pain in public. It means being pushed out of the way while you are walking or standing in line. It means to be made to feel unimportant, redundant and insignificant.

Being chronically unseen as a child is emotional neglect, which is a form of child abuse. It can look like being ignored by the caregiver when the child is in distress, not receiving affection or reassurance, being excluded, or being told that 'children should be seen, not heard', often implying that children's needs do not matter. These are all examples of child abuse that can have severe and adverse consequences on that person's physical and psychological development, including not feeling emotionally safe enough to form connections with other people.[1]

Being unseen can lead to an imbalance in our nervous system, increasing the fight-flight-freeze-fawn response, which causes us to feel very anxious about the safety and stability of our relationships. In severe cases of emotional neglect, in which the children's material needs (food, water, shelter) are met but the children are touch-starved and unseen, their brains form to look like the brains of people with epilepsy, because these individuals are always on high alert.[2]

Being unseen makes us feel unsafe, rejected and lonely. Worse, after being unseen continuously for a long time, we might begin to assume that we deserve to be treated this way, accepting mistreatment as the norm, or even as our fault.

Some people who experienced emotional abuse and neglect in childhood develop anxious attachment styles as adults. This means that they might frequently feel lonely and excessively worry about being abandoned, often feeling helpless and depressed in relationships as a result.[3] This type of loneliness is sometimes called *anaclitic depression*; however, it is essentially

1 Landry et al. (2022)
2 Eluvathingal, et al. (2006)
3 Reis & Grenyer (2002)

a traumatic response to emotional neglect. Because emotional neglect *IS* traumatic.

When we have been chronically neglected and unseen, the way Danielle has for many years with her friends and, previously to that, her parents, we might appear to have an unexpected reaction to a seemingly 'small' event – like a friend not responding to a text. And in these cases, we might ask ourselves, *Am I overreacting?* No, you are not. Because your feelings are not just about this event, the one that's happening in this very moment. They are about it being the thousandth event where it happened. Like Danielle, some people might have failed to reply to you, intentionally or unintentionally. And even though most people do not necessarily *intend* to hurt others, it doesn't mean that their actions do not hurt. For instance, someone might accidentally step on your foot, and although they didn't mean to hurt you, it doesn't mean that your pain is not real.

It is. Every ounce of it.

If you've ever felt like your emotional response was too extreme for the event that caused it – enraged about someone cutting you off on the road or cutting in front of you in a line, overwhelmed with anxiety because someone didn't respond to your text, frustrated or resentful when someone interrupted you – chances are that you felt unseen in that situation. And chances are that this one situation was not just one unique incident but rather the final drop into your patience bucket, which spilled years of unprocessed pain.

The rage, anxiety or devastation that you felt in those situations represent the culmination of years of being ignored, excluded or being made to feel unseen. It is the primal cry of the small innocent child within you, who is just fighting for survival.

And I'm here to tell you that the event you are upset about – it was not a 'small' event. None of them were.

You are a human being, and you deserved better. You deserve to be seen. I see you and I see your pain. You deserve to be noticed, to be acknowledged and to be treated with kindness and dignity.

Chapter 9
Lonely in a Relationship

'Joanna' came to see me two weeks after she and her husband, 'Steve', moved to California.

During her first two sessions, Joanna mostly just cried. I could see that she didn't have it in her to speak, so I didn't push her.

Over the twenty years of feeling unseen in her marriage, Joanna had lost her voice.

Not physically.

Physically, her vocal cords were intact. She could tell me her name, and her husband's name, and her dog's name. She could tell me which days of the week she was available for a session, and that she worked as a receptionist in an office.

But when I asked her how she was doing and what she hoped to work on in therapy, Joanna cried but couldn't say anything.

Joanna had lost the concept of *herself*, meaning that she couldn't answer any questions relating to her experiences. These questions included: 'How are you?', 'What is your favourite colour?' and 'What kind of food do you like to eat?' She could, however, answer factual questions, such as: 'What type of a car do you drive?', 'Which street do you live on?' and 'Which state did you live in before moving to California?'

I didn't push her.

For the first few sessions, we sat in gentle silence together, just me bearing witness to her pain, working to build her sense of emotional safety, letting her know that in this space, she wouldn't be rushed, pushed or judged.

After a month, Joanna began to talk a little bit more, but in a very limited way. She only spoke as a way of answering my questions and kept her answers as precise as possible.

She also would take anywhere between two and ten minutes to begin answering my questions, clearly weighing out the best way to respond.

When I asked her if she was being abused, Joanna shook her head and cried. She then shut down for the rest of the session.

The following month was the first time she volunteered the information without me asking first.

'That time when you asked me if I'm being abused,' Joanna said, fiddling with her handkerchief. 'Um, the thing is, Steve, he never hit me. He would never.'

I waited. I knew that prompting or interrupting her would cause her to shut down, so I just nodded.

It took her about three more minutes to find her words, 'He never hit me, but—' She burst out crying. 'I just feel like I don't exist when I'm around him. I don't want to exist when I'm around him.'

I nodded and waited for her to continue.

Joanna took a long breath. 'It's the first time I've said that out loud.' She swallowed. 'He gets up in the morning and doesn't wish me good morning. He just wants his breakfast and his coffee. I make them. He eats in silence, scrolling through his phone or answering work emails. Then he leaves without saying anything and goes to work.'

I nodded. 'And what do you do?'

She shook her head. 'I go to work, where I answer phones and emails. Sometimes I get yelled at, but no one ever asks me how I'm doing. I'm in charge of remembering everyone's birthdays at the office but no one ever remembers mine.'

Joanna's fists were shaking as she continued. 'And then I get home. I clean, I do the laundry. I make dinner.'

I nodded.

She continued, 'Last week Steve got mad at me because I didn't finish cooking dinner before he got home. He called me *lazy* because I work fewer hours than he does, but I feel like I never stop working.

'I cook and clean, I'm in charge of all the housework, but it's like I don't exist, and my work is invisible. And *I'm* also invisible.'

Tears were rolling down Joanna's cheeks now as she continued, 'And then he watches TV without asking me what I want to watch.'

She rolled her eyes. 'On weekends, sometimes we have sex. He doesn't ask me if I want to. He just does it. I don't even think it occurs to him that I might not want to. The time I said *no*, he got mad and yelled at me.'

She pounded her fist on the couch. 'And a few months ago, when you asked me how I was doing, I realised that it was the first time in about three years that someone asked me that and actually waited for me to answer.'

Like Joanna, many of us might feel unseen by our loved

ones. In relationships, being unseen might include any of the following:

- Stonewalling (punishment by rejection or ignoring)
- Ghosting (being abandoned without an explanation) or being ignored
- Gaslighting (manipulating someone to make them question their own reality)
- Being frequently interrupted or talked over
- Not getting credit for your work
- Being treated as a particular role you play rather than as a person (for example, being treated like a nurse, therapist, assistant or caretaker by friends and family members. In other words, being used for the services, skills or kindness you can provide to others and not being seen as a person)

In all these instances, we might feel not only invisible, but also erased. If this is happening to you, please know that the anger, sadness or frustration you are feeling is completely justified.

Feeling unseen strains relationships. It is one of the top reasons for relationship dissatisfaction and divorce, because feeling unseen leads to apathy and a deterioration of connection with our partners.

You deserve to be seen. You deserve to be treated with respect and kindness.

Chapter 10
Behind the Mask

There are many sensations we learn to attune to at an early age. For example, we learn to notice our bladder fullness to figure out when we need to use the bathroom. And as adults, we can then gauge when we need to take a break and use the bathroom before a long meeting or going on a road trip. If we are occasionally unable to notice our bladder either due to a medical issue or because we are too busy to notice it, we might have an accident. But if we frequently ignore our need to use the bathroom, we might develop kidney disease.

Hunger works the same way. If we are frequently ignoring our needs, we might develop headaches, stomach aches or vitamin deficiencies, which can wreak havoc on our health.

Loneliness works the same way. The more we ignore our needs, especially our need to be seen, the more distressed we become, and the bigger the impact on our health will be.

Several years ago, I was working with a young man, 'Nick', who was highly successful in his field. He was one of the top executives in his company and earned a very high salary. However, Nick was struggling with intense panic attacks. As we discussed his background, Nick opened up about having experienced physical, emotional and sexual abuse at the hands of his father as a small child.

'And there's something else,' he told me, his hands shaking in his lap. 'I have these *thoughts*. Terrifying thoughts.' He took a deep breath. 'I don't even want to tell you what they are because I'm afraid you'll have me arrested or hospitalised.'

He stopped talking and waited for me to respond, unblinking, and clearly holding his breath now.

I leaned forward in my chair. 'Let me tell you something about what happens to those of us who undergo abuse or witness violence. Our mind starts playing out every potential horrific scenario, to protect us. We might even imagine what would happen if we suddenly stabbed someone—'

'That's exactly what happens to me!' He interrupted. His eyes were full of hope now. 'When I'm in a restaurant, I imagine stabbing my date. Or a waiter.'

'And do you actually want to do it?' I asked him.

'Oh, God, no!' he said, his eyes wide. 'I even reduced how often I go to the restaurant. I just go for walks with my dates most of the time now. And if I ever go to a restaurant, I make sure I order a salad, not a steak, so that they don't bring out one of those big knives to the table. What is wrong with me?'

I smiled at him. 'Nick, listen to me. There's nothing wrong with you. You are having a natural reaction to the horrific events that you've been through. People with trauma history, and also people with OCD, even if they'd never experienced trauma, might struggle with intrusive thoughts about harming other people, not because they want to, but precisely because they do not. People with trauma, OCD and anxiety might fear harming other people but never actually do. People who actually harm other people don't worry about doing so.'

Nick leaned back and stared at me. 'Really?'

'Really.' I nodded.

He smiled. 'This is the first time I've ever felt *normal*. Whatever that means. I've always thought I had to wear this *mask*, you know?'

I did know.

I DO know.

We all wear metaphorical masks. You know the ones I'm talking about:

Hi. How are you?

I'm fine. How are you?

These are the *masked scripts* most of us have rehearsed since we began speaking.

And I don't know about you, but I'm never *fine*. I'm always worried about something, always managing a million things, feeling overwhelmed and burned out.

And I think most of us have been conditioned to wear these *I am fine* masks as a kind of a universal lie.

Whether you're a trauma survivor like Nick or you are like my other client, 'Melissa,' a new mom, who is going through postpartum depression and suicide-related thoughts, or 'Jessica,' who is working two jobs while taking care of her two-year-old son, as well as her husband who is going through cancer, you might tell people that you're 'fine' when you clearly do not feel that way.

You might be going through a painful divorce, a break-up, feel cut off from your friends or family members, or feel unseen in your gender expression. You might be struggling with depression, anxiety, an eating disorder or have trouble feeling like you belong.

And in all of these situations, you will not feel *fine*. You will likely feel angry, scared, overwhelmed and exhausted. And how could you not feel that way? Anyone in your situation would feel the way you do. The people who invalidate you, make you feel unseen, and tell you to *get over it* might tell you that they wouldn't feel the same way, but they are kidding themselves. If they had all your history and your experiences, they would feel the same way you are feeling right now.

Anybody would.

To be seen, to be truly seen, takes a lot of courage because it is a very vulnerable process.

In her amazing book *Daring Greatly*, Brené Brown differentiates between *fitting in* and *belonging*.[1] Essentially, *fitting in* refers to trying to change or hide who you are to try to fit with a particular group. *Belonging*, on the other hand, means allowing ourselves to be truly seen by others. Belonging allows us to be loved and accepted unconditionally without any masks.

Many of us wear metaphorical masks because we believe that we are more likely to fit in with them than without them. Except that's not how it works. Because you see, the very thing you're trying to hide – the truth about who you are – that's the most lovable part of you.

1 Brown (2015)

Chances are that you have, at times, felt closer to people after you'd learned something personal about them, especially if you could relate to it yourself. And chances are that the more you got to know someone you consider to be a deep and kind person, the more you probably have grown to care about them.

Of course, there might be times when you feel so overwhelmed and exhausted that you mask or say that you are 'fine' just because you do not have the time or the energy to do otherwise. And that's perfectly okay. Sometimes that's exactly what we need to do. Just know that when you are ready, you do not have to mask if you do not want to. For most people you will meet, the more they see *you*, the *truer you*, the more they will love you. And the ones who do not care to see *the real you* aren't your people.

You deserve to be seen. You deserve to be true to who you are. Because who you truly are matters. Who you truly are is the most lovable part of you.

Chapter 11
Ghosting

One of my past clients, 'Kelly', came to one of our weekly sessions in tears.

She had been dating her partner, 'Michael', for five months, and the two were making plans for the holidays. Then, suddenly, Michael cancelled one of their dates and asked her to hold off booking their holiday trip.

Kelly was confused and texted to ask him if everything was all right, but Michael didn't respond. After a few days, Kelly attempted to call him, only to discover that Michael had blocked her on his phone and all social media.

'I just don't understand,' Kelly said, dabbing her eyes with a tissue. 'What did I do wrong? Why did he just disappear like that?'

This type of a sudden ending of all communication without providing any warning or a reason is called *ghosting*. Ghosting creates a rupture, a loss. It is a type of abandonment. Ghosting is different from a regular break-up because it leaves countless unanswered questions that can prolong our healing process. It's cruel and cowardly to abandon someone without any warning or an explanation unless it is physically or emotionally unsafe for the other person to do so.

Whether it's a romantic relationship or a friendship,

ghosting feels like a confusing combination of a break-up and grief. On the one hand, it feels like the other person has died, but on the other hand, we might not have the support and the grieving rituals that would normally be available to us when someone has passed away.

Ghosting is, in fact, a loss, and for some people it can be a very traumatic one. There is a term for this type of an experience – ambiguous loss. Ambiguous loss occurs when someone has suddenly (or over time) disappeared from our life, but they are still alive.[1] Examples of ambiguous losses include ghosting, abandonment, rejection by family or a community (a church, for example), as well as suddenly being fired or laid off, going through a break-up or a divorce, or being kicked out of your friendship group.

In all of these cases, we might feel unseen and, in some instances, discarded, left with thousands of unanswered questions. We might be going through old conversations to try to understand what happened. We might try pleading with the other person, begging them to reconsider, or asking mutual friends for answers. These are all normal responses to your grief. We plead for connection when we feel a sudden disconnection.

The grief you feel in these cases is real and your feelings, whether you feel hurt, angry, lonely, confused or scared, are all valid, and anyone in your situation would feel the same way.

To be suddenly abandoned in this way is hard enough. However, many (well-meaning) people in our lives might advise

1 Scarlet (2021)

us to 'just get over it', to 'focus on the positive' and to 'stop thinking about it'.

This kind of invalidation can make us feel even lonelier and even more unseen.

When I was in college, I experienced ghosting as well. My friend 'Tina' and I were very close and either hung out or talked on the phone every day. Suddenly, our communication began to fade. We went from daily phone calls to barely speaking. This was very abrupt and when I asked her about it, Tina said she was 'just busy' but our conversations were less warm than they had been. In fact, they had become so superficial that I felt like I was talking to a stranger.

This lasted a year.

One day, I called her on our scheduled time to talk and she didn't pick up. I left a voicemail asking if she could please call when she was able.

She messaged me the next day, saying that she didn't get my call and asked if we could reschedule but didn't give me alternative options. I sent her a few options, but she didn't respond.

The following week, I ran into a mutual friend who told me that Tina was having a game night at her house the night that I called. When her phone rang, she showed everyone that it was me calling, and then told them all how annoyed she was that I was calling her.

Tina had lied to me for over a year, telling me she was still interested in our friendship instead of telling me the truth. And even though my intuition told me that something wasn't right and that she wasn't being truthful, I took her at her word.

What I have learned over the years is that some people pull away from friendships for their own reasons. Sadly, they might mistakenly believe that by not telling you that they don't want to be friends any more, they are being kind, when in fact, they're leaving you in the dark with unanswered questions.

If this happens to you, please know this isn't about anything you did. It's about what they need and what they are going through. It is because they don't currently have the skills, the courage or the ability to tell you the truth.

I learned years later that, at the time Tina started pulling away from me, she had been cheating on her partner and was experimenting with drugs. I also learned that she pulled away from many of her closest friends and family members during the following few years, most likely because she was in a lot of pain and feared being judged.

Tina and I have rekindled our friendship over the years, but it will never be what it once was, and that's okay. The way that I personally got to being 'okay' with it was to allow myself to feel both seemingly conflicting emotions that I experienced when Tina and I reunited – hurt and empathy. I understood that her choices were not about me, and I felt for her. And I also allowed myself to feel the pain that her actions brought up in me. By making space for both of these emotions, I was able to make space for our friendship as well.

If you feel that a loved one is pulling away, please know that their reasons are more likely to do with their own shame and trauma than with you. Just like Kelly, whose partner pulled away from her without an explanation, chances are that the person who ghosted you or abandoned you in some way did so in order to avoid the shame and guilt that they would have felt by being direct and honest with you.

Your pain is valid even if you can empathise and understand why someone hurt you. It was never about you. It was about them not having the skills or the courage to tell you the truth. And if they will never apologise or explain why they hurt you, then let me say that I am so sorry that they did that. It's not okay and you deserved better. You still do.

Chapter 12
Bargaining

It was February 2022. I was gut wrenched with what was happening in my home country, with what my friends and family were going through. As a Ukrainian native and grandchild of four Holocaust survivors, the Russian invasion of Ukraine shook me to my core. I started having nightmares. I could barely sleep. I was checking the news all the time, holding my breath while checking on my friends and family back home.

One of my closest friends, 'Layla', texted me about three days after the start of the war. She said that she'd been feeling overwhelmed and needed some space from our friendship and didn't have much time to give right now.

I told myself, *She's just setting a boundary. It's great that she's letting me know what she needs.*

I was confused since I hadn't texted her much since the war began, other than to cancel our plans because I needed to focus on my friends and family. I hadn't relied on her nor asked for her support.

I responded with, 'Yes, of course, no problem. I hope you're able to get some rest. I'm here if there's anything you need.'

But my anxiety began to spiral. It generated thoughts like, *I must have done something wrong, and that's why she's pulling away.*

But my logical brain argued that everything was fine. After all, we spent nearly every weekend together. We talked about everything. We met each other's families and spent holidays and birthdays together.

Plus, I reminded myself, *Layla is a fantastic communicator. If something is wrong, she'll say something. She won't leave without an explanation.*

I told myself that Layla just needed a few weeks and would reach out to me when she was ready.

In the meantime, the war in my home country raged on and I struggled to cope. I poured all my time and efforts into offering any support possible, including teaching workshops to Ukrainian psychologists, teaching Psychological First Aid courses to Ukrainian volunteers, and offering pro bono therapy to Ukrainian refugees.

'You're supporting so many people. Who is supporting you?' my therapist asked me.

That's when I realised that it had been a month since Layla reached out.

My denial of what was happening turned to anger. *How could she do that?*

But the anger faded and quickly turned into my obsessive need for understanding and certainty.

As I was trying to manage my own grief that my home country was being invaded, I was also trying to make sense of what had happened between Layla and me.

I couldn't sleep at night, replaying our old conversations.

Was it because I called her twice in one day? I asked myself.

I'd called to cancel our plans because I was heading out to a #StandWithUkraine demonstration. She didn't pick up, so I called again to leave a message. That was the same day she'd asked for some space.

Was it because I cancelled our plans?

A little over two months after Layla asked me for space, I texted her. I asked if we could talk about what happened, but also let her know that there was no rush to respond, and that she did not have to respond at all if she did not want to.

But of course, I was holding my breath, and rereading the message I sent for days, hoping to hear back.

And I did.

A few days later, Layla texted me, thanking me for our friendship but stating that she didn't think our friendship was a good fit.

A million questions went through my mind. *Why? What did I do wrong? Which of my actions caused this?*

I kept searching my mind for the *right* answer until my therapist said, 'It sounds like you're grieving.'

'Yes, of course I'm grieving,' I said. 'I really cared about this friendship, and so it makes sense that I'm grieving.'

'And which stage of grief are you in right now?' she asked.

I thought about the Kübler-Ross stages of grief model: Denial, Anger, Bargaining, Depression and Acceptance.[1] Of course, these stages aren't linear, meaning that we do not necessarily experience them in this exact order, and we might cycle

1 Kübler-Ross (1973)

through them multiple times. These stages also were designed for people who are dying, not for the bereaved, but they can still help to explain some of the emotions we are feeling.

'Let's see,' I said, 'I'm not in denial. I'm past anger.' I shrugged. 'I don't know. I just want to understand what happened. I want to have closure.'

'And what do you think this type of understanding will bring you?' my therapist asked.

My lips moved before I could think about it: 'A way out of this pain.'

As soon as I said it, I felt the chill of understanding all over my body.

'I'm in the bargaining stage,' I said.

My therapist nodded.

My mind told me that if I could just figure out what happened, I wouldn't feel this way. But that's not true.

The reality is that I will never know the truth about what happened. And the fact is that it's none of my business why Layla decided to end our friendship. It was her decision and she's allowed to decide what's best for her.

And it is also true that it hurt. It hurt like hell.

As I continued processing this event, I realised that I was making this experience about me and not about Layla. I let my trauma and my ego narrate the interpretations of what might have possibly happened, getting stuck in the bargaining stage.

But the moment I was able to name this experience, *bargaining*, and acknowledge what was happening, I started to focus on healing instead of trying to figure out why. This allowed me to make space for my feelings and to recognise that I had them because Layla meant a lot to me.

For some of us, bargaining is a way that we might try to make sense of a devastating loss, such as abandonment by a loved one. One of my clients, let's call her 'Christy', shared that her father abandoned her family when she was eight years old.

'I came home from school one day and he was gone,' she told me. 'His clothes were gone, his car was gone, he was just ... gone. He didn't say goodbye. He didn't say anything to me, my mother or my brothers. He just left.'

Like many people whose loved ones abandoned them at a young age, Christy developed trauma symptoms after this loss.

'I kept asking myself, What did I do wrong?' Christy said. 'I had nightmares of him driving away, even though I never actually saw him leave. And then when I got older and started dating, I was terrified of my partner leaving me. Anytime he would get upset, my body felt like I couldn't breathe. The terror was so strong, that I would freeze and shut down.'

Many people who were abandoned by a loved one, including people who were orphaned and adoptees, are more likely to experience trauma symptoms, including anxiety and depression around any potential abandonment by loved ones in the future.[2] This is because abandonment is, in itself, traumatic. Whether it is abandonment by a parent, a partner, a close friend or a mentor, abandonment hurts at the core of our experience.

The feelings that we feel as a result are grief.

2 Whetten, et al. (2011).

Excruciating, heart-wrenching grief.

The questions we ask, trying to figure out why, that's bargaining. And these tears you shed when you feel the pain, that's your heart mending itself.

Let it heal.

Chapter 13
Social Exclusion

Jennifer has been feeling lonely ever since she was a small child. Her parents and older brother would wait for her to go to sleep and then play games that she wasn't allowed to partake in, even if she wanted to. When Jennifer would cry because she felt lonely, she was labelled a troublemaker, and was punished.

At school, Jennifer was bullied and ostracised for her social anxiety. For most of her childhood, Jennifer was left to play by herself. She would self-soothe by watching *Star Wars* and *Star Trek*, their characters becoming her surrogate friends over time.

Because we are wired for connection, the pain of disconnection doesn't just feel hurtful, it can be harmful to our health. Research studies analysing the effects of social exclusion show that when we experience even the smallest act of intentional exclusion, we are likely to experience heightened physical and emotional pain.

In one study, a virtual ball-tossing game was created, and research participants were either included (where the other participants passed the ball to them) or excluded (where the other virtual players did not pass the ball to the participant). When the participants were excluded, the activation of the pain centres of their brain was significantly higher than when they were included, as measured by the fMRI.[1] This means that people who were excluded in this virtual ball-tossing game experienced more physical and emotional distress than participants who were included in the game.

Clearly, being excluded, just as Jennifer was, leads to high amounts of emotional and physical pain and suffering. This is why most of us would do just about anything not to feel excluded or ignored. Little kids sometimes misbehave, not out of spite, but because they don't know how else to meet their vital need of connection and belonging – negative attention is still better than no attention.

As adults, we do it too – when we feel excluded, we can become defensive, passive-aggressive or shut down. For example, someone who doesn't get invited to a social event might claim that they didn't want to go in the first place. We might also rely on substances, overwork or perfectionism, anything just to avoid feeling lonely and excluded.

In some cases, we might join groups that are unhealthy but remain in those communities or relationships because we often don't trust our ability to handle loneliness. And when we step away from the abuse and the neglect we've endured, that's when the healing starts. Because the only way out of this kind of pain is through it.

As an adult, Jennifer's loneliness meant she was desperately trying to survive. She repeatedly tried being friends with different people only to have them bully and threaten her. In

---

1 Eisenberger (2012); Eisenberger, et al. (2006)

looking for any form of a connection, Jennifer joined a group that she initially believed to be a religious group. She joined because they promised her that she would never be alone again. She realised later that this group was a cult and over time, she was abused and alienated there as well.

When she was finally able to leave, Jennifer once again found refuge in *Star Wars* and social media. She found posts and videos that other people shared about their experiences with loneliness and about finding a sense of connection through pop culture. Because of that, Jennifer began making new friends and forming connections based around conversations about loneliness and fictional characters.

'If I could have one thing,' Jennifer said, 'it would be that people would see the damage that is caused by alienating people and making them feel like they don't matter. I was pushed to nearly killing myself because of the hopelessness of my situation. I thought the grief would destroy me. I remember days and days of feeling like my heartbreak would actually stop my heart.'

I asked Jennifer what she would say to her younger self if she could talk to her.

She said, 'I would hug my younger self and say, *You are going to be okay. You will create thousands of smiles, help heal dozens of hearts and never stop hearing laughter. Just hold on, you've got this.*'

Like Jennifer, everyone has their own story of loneliness, trauma and exclusion. And it is when we share these stories with other people with similar experiences that we are likely to find the path to our own healing. Sometimes the people living next door to you, the people standing next to you on the elevator, the people standing in line behind you at the grocery store, are the people whose hearts are breaking, the people who could use your smile, your kindness and your compassion. Sometimes the person you might assume to be more resilient than you might be the one struggling with severe loneliness and wishing that someone like you would start the conversation they don't have the courage to begin. And it's precisely through conversations that hearts begin to heal, and miracles take place.

Chapter 14
Invisible Labour

One of my clients, 'Leah', reported that she was really frustrated with her husband. Let's call him 'John'.

Leah was eight months pregnant with her second child while working full time as an accountant and taking care of her toddler.

'We work the same number of hours,' Leah said about John, 'but when he comes home, he says that he's tired and needs to rest.'

'And what do you need?' I asked.

'I need some help,' Leah said. 'When I get home, I cook, I clean, I do the laundry, all while entertaining our son.'

'And what does your husband do?'

'He plays with our son for a few minutes and then says that he needs to relax and turns on the TV. In the meantime, I feed the baby, I do the bath time, and I put him to bed.'

'That's a lot of work,' I said.

'It is,' Leah said. 'And when I try to ask John to help more, he says that he got groceries the previous week. In the meantime, I work full time, just like he does, but feel like a single mom most of the time.'

Leah is one of countless people burned out by invisible labour.

Invisible labour refers to the work that many people do, and others fail to recognise. Housework is an example of that. Many partners, especially women (although people of all sexes and gender identities might experience this), engage in countless tasks that their partner does not notice.

As a result, the partner who completes all the work, like Leah, will likely feel not only unseen, but also resentful of the other partner. Invisible labour not only feels lonely, but it also breeds resentment and rupture in relationships. People who complete the invisible labour without acknowledgement or support might essentially feel as if their partner is saying, 'I don't appreciate you. Your work doesn't matter. What you do is not important.'

A similar experience that many people go through is the *mental load*. Mental load refers to juggling many appointments and responsibilities in one's mind. Leah shared that she carried a heavy mental load in terms of remembering all the groceries, bills and doctor's appointments.

'What makes it worse,' she said, 'is that it's not only my own responsibilities I carry. I carry them for John, too. I have to remind him to pay the electric bill every month and then I have to follow up to see if he did it because he forgot a few times. We ended up having to pay late fees. I literally have to manage everything and it's exhausting.'

'Have you talked to John about that?' I asked.

Leah scoffed. 'I did. And you know what he said? He said that he's not worried about missing payments because he knows that if he forgets, I'll remind him.'

'How did you feel when he said that?' I asked.

'So mad! It feels like I have to do absolutely everything. And I feel so alone in all of it.' She furrowed her eyebrows. 'I didn't realise how angry I was until just now. These seem to be such inconsequential issues, but they don't feel small. I don't know how to explain it to him.'

What many people in these situations, like Leah, often fail to understand is that the issue isn't about 'one small thing'. The issue is that it's about an accumulation of thousands of 'small things' that chip away at your connection with your partner and your trust in them.

And after a few thousand cracks, that dam is going to burst.

Your labour matters, whether the people around you see it or not. You deserve to get the help and the support that you need. You deserve to have your efforts recognised. You deserve to be seen.

Chapter 15
What Can You Do if You Are Feeling Unseen?

Although it is not uncommon to feel unseen, it is important to acknowledge that it is happening, so that you can practise supporting yourself through it or advocate for yourself the same way you would advocate for a loved one in this situation. Here are some steps to try out.

1. Name it: 'I'm feeling unseen.' Naming your experience can allow you to better navigate the situation. Name any emotions that you feel as a result, as well. For example, 'I feel angry, frustrated, hurt and lonely.'

2. Feel it: Notice where in your body you're feeling these emotions. For example, you might notice that you're holding a lot of tension in your shoulders or that your chest feels tight. Perhaps your stomach feels heavy, nauseated or has a 'drop' feeling, as if you're about to go down a rollercoaster. Maybe your jaw is clenched, or your arms or legs feel tight. Maybe there's a pressure on the top of your head. Maybe your thoughts are racing like bees in a beehive.

Notice whatever you're feeling. Just notice it. Observe your own pain because you deserve to be seen.

I'm right here in your corner. I'm here to remind you that

your frustration is valid. Anyone in your situation would feel this way. It's unfair and you deserve better.

3. Breathe into it: Pick one of the areas where you felt your emotions, for example, as a tightness in your chest. Then set a timer on your phone or another device for one minute. If you don't have a timer, you can count to sixty either silently or out loud for this exercise.

And for one minute, focus on just this one area and breathe. Take slow, comfortable breaths, not pushing or straining your breath. Imagine the area you're focusing on relaxing and settling down with each exhale.

Sometimes when we're frustrated, we need to cry. If tears come, let them come. Don't fight them. The tears are good. This is you healing.

Once the minute is up, switch to one of the other areas where you felt your emotions and repeat this exercise while focusing on this new area (such as nausea in your stomach) for one minute. Repeat this exercise for each of the areas you identified. Feel free to do this exercise again for a particular area if you need to.

This exercise is about allowing you to soothe. It is not going to take away your anger, frustration or hurt. You need those. These emotions are data points. They tell you that you have an unmet need, such as the need to be seen and valued.

And so, instead of getting rid of your emotions, this exercise is meant to soothe your body, as a way of giving you the support that you need to get through this experience.

In later chapters, we will learn steps for getting your needs met, such as being assertive and setting boundaries. Before we get there, let's focus on getting you all the support that you need right now.

4. Vent and process: In addition to practising the three steps we discussed in this chapter so far, see if you can practise letting out some steam. Is there a friend or a therapist you can reach out to who will listen to you vent? If you don't have a trusted friend or a therapist to turn to, see if you can vent about how you're feeling by writing it out on a piece of paper or on your phone, by using a voice recorder on your phone or simply by venting out loud in a safe space by yourself.

These exercises are just for you, so there's no reason to make them 'perfect'. Whichever of these techniques you end up using, please know that you're not alone. It makes sense that you feel the way that you do. Anyone with your history would feel the same way in this situation. You matter and you deserve to be seen and cared for.

TAKE AWAYS

- Remember that everyone has felt unseen at times.
- Research shows feeling seen is a valid, real, physical need.
- Being ghosted (sudden ending of all communication without providing any warning) is a valid form of loss.
- Feeling unseen can result in a rupture of relationships; it is a disruption of trust.
- If you are feeling sad, angry, furious or anxious over a seemingly 'small' event, it is due to an accumulation, likely of years, of emotional abandonment or invalidation by other people.
- If you feel unseen, you can practise self-soothing through the following steps:
    1. Name your experience
    2. Feel it in your body
    3. Breathe into it
    4. Vent about it and process it
- You deserve to be seen when you're grieving, and you can advocate for the ways you want to be supported.
- You are not 'asking for too much'. You are not 'overreacting'. You are expressing a valid need. You deserve to be seen.

PART 3:
Unheard

Chapter 16
Undate

'You shouldn't be alone at a time like this,' 'Anthony' said to me over the phone after learning that my grandmother had died. He wanted me to meet him in our local park to go on a walk together.

I was flipping through my family's dark blue photo album in my living room when he called. I swallowed, looking at an old, black-and-white picture of my grandparents, both of them now gone.

'You still there?' he asked.

I sighed. 'Yes, sorry. Um, okay. So long as you understand that it's not a date.'

'Yes, of course. I just want to support you,' he said.

When we met up at Owl's Head Park in Brooklyn, Anthony hugged me and offered his condolences again.

We sat together on the green wooden bench, overlooking the bay and the distant Manhattan skyline. He put his arm around me and said, 'I'm really glad we're finally having this date.'

I stifled a scream. *Why does this keep happening to me? Did I do something to make him think it was a date?*

I had insisted that this meeting was not a date largely because of the numerous surprise 'undates' I'd found myself on in the past.

My mind flashed to my high-school lab partner, 'Glen', who invited me to his house to work on our school project. When I went over, he introduced me to his parents as his girlfriend.

I was speechless, too stunned to correct him in front of his parents. And when they slipped away to the kitchen, I asked him, 'What is this? Glen, I'm not your girlfriend. I have a boyfriend. You met him, remember?'

He shrugged. 'It doesn't matter. In your reality, you have another boyfriend. In mine, you're my girlfriend. What's the harm if no one gets hurt?'

I felt too uncomfortable to say what I was silently screaming in my mind: *Me! I'm getting harmed!* Instead, I didn't say anything at all.

Over the years, I'd heard many stories just like this from both clients and friends. At best, these situations would lead to ultimatums, such as, 'If you won't go out with me, I won't be your friend', leaving the person either to be pressured into a relationship they didn't want to be in or mourning the loss of a friendship they didn't realise was conditional. At worst, the person who did not wish to enter a relationship with the other individual may find themselves assaulted or killed.

This is the reality that many people live in, especially those who identify as women or as feminine.

If you feel pressured to do something you don't want to do and are starting to get frustrated, you aren't overreacting.

You are not exaggerating.

You're screaming to be heard.

I hear you. And your voice matters.

Chapter 17
'I'm Not Deaf, I'm an Immigrant'

When I was in my late twenties, my partner's grandmother passed away. The two of us flew out to St Louis, Missouri, to attend the funeral.

I held my partner's hand as we stood next to his parents in the funeral home and greeted those who arrived to say their final farewells. It was an open casket, and we all whispered, keeping our voices as quiet as possible as a sign of respect until—

'HI, I'M LARRY!' a loud voice boomed over me.

I spun around to face a middle-aged, thin, white, bald man, wearing a grey suit and a striped tie.

He stuck out his hand to me, smiling and shouting, as if I were on the opposite end of a football field, while gesticulating with his hands something that most certainly was not any form of a sign language. 'I KNOW YOU ARE FROM THE UKRAINE. HOW ARE YOU?'

I felt my cheeks blush. *What do I tell him? Do I tell him he's being rude by shouting at a funeral? Do I tell him he's being xenophobic by assuming I don't speak English? Do I tell him that it's just Ukraine, not THE Ukraine?*

Do I tell him that I'm not hard of hearing and he does not need to shout, nor should he be gesticulating wildly as if playing charades while buzzed on coffee? And maybe more importantly, *How do I handle this so as not to detract attention from what's important, the fact that we're at a funeral and his behaviour is disrespectful to my partner's family?*

I chose the politest approach I could think of. I took a step closer to him, forced a polite smile, shook his hand, and whispered, 'Nice to meet you, Larry. I speak English. I'm fluent, actually.'

His smile shaped into a nervous grin. He seemed to be processing this information.

Please don't bring attention to me again. Please.

'HOW DO YOU LIKE AMERICA? IS IT BETTER THAN LIFE IN THE UKRAINE?' Larry shouted and gesticulated again, so close to my face that I could smell his breath.

'In my culture, it is not polite to speak with a raised voice at a funeral,' I whispered and quietly walked away.

I can only hope that he heard me, and I don't mean physically.

Sadly, xenophobia, racism and other forms of discrimination exist and happen every day. If it happens to you, please know that you have every right to be angry and you have every right to step away from that environment. You matter and you deserve better.

Chapter 18
What Does it Mean to be Unheard?

It wasn't the panic attacks that derailed 'Stephanie's' life. It was her family's reactions to them.

'It's like everyone is suddenly an expert in my condition even though none of them have ever had panic attacks,' she told me in one of our sessions. 'My husband's telling me that I need to drink more water, my sister is telling me to pray more, and my mom is telling me to just not think about it.'

'Oof. That sounds really frustrating,' I said.

'So frustrating! All they are doing is giving me unsolicited advice instead of really listening to me.'

'What would have been a more helpful response from them?' I asked.

Stephanie thought about it. 'I guess asking me to tell them what my experience is. And then just validating me. Just saying that it sounds really hard what I'm going through, and to say they are here for me.'

'I hear you,' I said. 'And it *is* hard. And I can hear how overwhelming and challenging this has been. I'm here in your corner and we will get through this together.'

Her eyes welled with tears. 'Thank you. That's literally all I needed to hear.'

Feeling unheard refers not only to someone not understanding you, but also to someone invalidating you or arguing with you about your own experience.

The most extreme form of being unheard is *gaslighting*, in which one person intentionally persuades the other that they didn't see, hear or experience something the way that they know they did.

Let's say that a woman saw her husband kiss someone else and then she confronted him about it. If her husband insisted that it didn't happen and that she must have just 'imagined it', this would be an example of gaslighting. Gaslighting causes feelings of confusion, as well as frequently questioning your own experiences, treading gently when trying to explain yourself and over-rehearsing how you might explain something to someone because you often feel dismissed and unheard. The main difference between gaslighting and unskilful communication is that gaslighting is intentional. The gaslighter will purposely twist the facts to make someone doubt themselves, whereas an unskilful communicator might genuinely try to understand the other person but might not have the best skills to meet their needs.

For example, 'Rachel' was sexually abused by her father for many years when she was a small child. In school, Rachel was always a high achiever but struggled to connect with kids her own age. In adulthood, she experienced severe brain fog, irritability and self-isolation. When she tried confronting her father in her adulthood, thinking that she could get closure by receiving his apology, her father denied it ever happened.

After her father's gaslighting, Rachel's brain fog became significantly worse. Eventually, Rachel needed to quit her job because of the severity of her symptoms. Despite all medical tests coming back negative, Rachel's brain fog persisted.

When we started to work together in treatment, we explored the possibility that her brain fog might be a reaction to severe trauma and also to the loneliness of her experience. Together, we also explored the idea that her experience was valid even if her perpetrator did not give her the closure she needed. Because even if your abuser denies your reality (as is often the case) and does not give you the validation that you need, this does not make your experience any less real. You do not have to wait for the abuser to validate you or agree with you to start healing. Your experience was always real and your feelings about it are valid.

Rachel and I worked on her sharing her story – first one-on-one in therapy, then with her partner, and then in a sexual abuse support group. As she shared her story over time with the people in her life and found others who had similar experiences, her brain fog began to lift, and she found herself ready to work again. By sharing her own story, Rachel was able to take ownership of it. She was able to take her power back, rather than waiting for her perpetrator to admit to what he did to her.

If something like this has ever happened to you, if you were abused, assaulted or mistreated in any way, please know that your pain and your story are valid even if your perpetrator never hears you. I hear you. And other people will too. You deserve to be heard.

Although gaslighting is not uncommon, most of the time people don't hear us because they lack the skills they need to actively listen. In addition, some people who are struggling with loneliness, depression or grief might not have the emotional resources to face their own experiences and, as a result, will not be able to hear others who are dealing the same difficulties as well.

Unfortunately, it is often true that those who are struggling the most get the least amount of support from people closest to them. Those who've lost a loved one might suddenly find themselves abandoned by their dearest friends or given very unhelpful advice, such as, 'everything happens for a reason' or 'this was so long ago, you need to let it go' or 'you need to be strong'.

Survivors of sexual assault, narcissistic abuse, intimate partner violence or other painful experiences are often shamed by their loved ones for 'letting it happen' or for 'not leaving sooner'. These are all examples of being unheard.

Feeling unheard perpetuates feelings of loneliness because it makes us believe that our experiences are invalid, that we deserved them, or that we are alone in going through them. In reality, it's not that you are the only one who feels this way, it's that you are the one who is brave enough to tell the truth.

A well-known fairy tale, *The Emperor's New Clothes* by Hans Christian Andersen, tells a story of two men who offer to make the most exquisite robes for a vain emperor, telling him that fools will not be able to see his robes, but smart people will.

The emperor agrees. And when the men show him the finished robes, the emperor doesn't see them. Fearing being seen as a fool, the emperor praises the men and decides to parade around town in his new robes.

All around town, the people praise the emperor's clothes, so that they do not appear to be fools.

Only a small child is brave enough to say, 'But the emperor's got no clothes.'

The people around us often fall into patterns that make their lives feel safe and predictable. Like the little child in the story, you too might be the only one brave enough to tell the truth while everyone else might be parroting what they hear others say around them for the fear of looking foolish. You were the one who was brave enough to tell the truth. You were always the brave one.

Learning about trauma, loneliness and emotions takes a lot of courage because it's painful and uncomfortable. Many people find it easier to give advice and shut the door.

This means that whenever you feel unheard, you aren't wrong. You are right.

Five Steps Technique

If other people aren't doing enough to hear and validate you, let's practise getting your needs met in other ways.

This is an exercise that's built on the one you learned in the previous section. This exercise will appear in a number of sections in the book because practising it repeatedly tends to be more helpful than only practising it once:

1. Name it: Do you feel unheard? Which emotions do you feel right now? Do you feel angry? Frustrated? Empty? Numb? Devastated?

2. Feel it: Notice where in your body you're feeling these emotions.

3. Breathe into them: Take one minute to breathe into each

109

area where you feel these emotions. Shake them out if you need to – shake out your arms, legs or shoulders to loosen up some of the tension you might be holding in these areas.

4. Vent: Vent to a friend, talk to a therapist, write it out on a piece of paper or vent out loud in a safe space. Allow yourself to express how you feel.

5. What do you need to hear: This is a new step. Meeting your own needs is just as important as acknowledging your needs. Think about what words of support and encouragement you really need to hear. Say them or write them out.

Try saying it to yourself. Validate yourself.

You deserve to be heard.

Chapter 19
Screaming into the Void

'Chris' lost his father to cancer when he was thirteen years old.

'My uncle pulled me aside at the funeral and told me that I had to "man up" and to "be strong" for my mom,' Chris told me in one of our initial sessions. 'We hadn't even buried him yet, and my relatives were already dictating how I was supposed to feel.'

'I'm so sorry, Chris. It was hard enough to lose your dad but to then have family members invalidate your feelings – that's really hard.'

He nodded. 'I felt like I was all alone in this. My mom shut down. She never wanted to talk about him; said it was too painful. My sister was too young to understand what was happening. And none of my school friends could relate.'

He took a big breath. 'It's hard, you know, when everyone else I knew had a dad and I didn't. Father's Day sucks for me to this day. Holidays have become hard in general. And it's like no one gets it, not really. Not unless they've been through it.'

'It sounds really lonely,' I said.

He nodded. 'It is. When I try to talk to my family members about him, they tell me that I need to move on. When I try talking to my friends, they don't hear me. They just say that my dad wouldn't have wanted me to be sad for so long.'

'Oof. So invalidating,' I said. 'What do you say to them?'

Chris looked up at me. 'Who? My friends? Nothing. I don't say anything. There's no point. They won't understand.'

'And if you could – if you could explain it to them, what do you WISH they could understand?'

Chris took another breath before answering, 'I'd tell them that they didn't even know my dad. I barely knew my dad. He worked a lot, he travelled for work, and then he got sick. And I hate that I barely knew him. And there's a part of me that's mad at him for leaving, and mostly, I'm mad at myself for not spending more time with him.

'I'd tell them that I'm angry at my mom for not being there for me. But mostly, I'd tell them that I feel like no one ever tries to understand what I go through. They just want to *fix* how I feel. And on most days, I just want to scream into the void, but I feel like the void isn't listening either.'

Being unheard in any situation is very painful. Being unheard when you're going through grief or trauma can feel like a betrayal. And in many ways, it is – an unintentional betrayal. You were likely counting on your loved ones to have your back and they didn't hear you, or worse, didn't want to hear you. Situations like these can cause a rupture in trust and in relationships. Luckily, this rupture can be mended if everyone is willing to try.

One way to mend a rupture if you are not being heard is to write out what you would like the other person to understand. I usually recommend that people write one letter, completely uncensored, letting all their feelings out, without worrying about grammar or whether it makes sense. This letter is just for you. You can shred it or burn it afterward, but it's important that you write this version first, so that you can be heard by the most important witness – yourself.

Next, if you'd like, feel free to write another letter, this one with an intention of giving it to the other person. Even with the most poised letter, there is a chance that you won't be heard. If you are not getting your needs met, it's okay to step away and take care of yourself (we will review some ways of caring for yourself in Part 5).

In the meantime, focus on what you need. You deserve it.

Chapter 20
Ableist Oppression

My colleague 'Tammy' struggles with chronic migraines. One day when she was a teenager, Tammy woke up with a horrific migraine and was barely able to lift her head. She called her boss and requested to take a sick day.

However, her boss said that if Tammy didn't come in, she'd be fired because the company was short staffed. She then proceeded to tell Tammy to 'just pop an aspirin and come in'.

When Tammy tried to explain how excruciating her migraines are, her boss raised her voice: 'Either come in or you're fired.'

Tammy forced herself to get to work despite the horrific pain she was feeling. She wore her sunglasses as a way to make her migraine more manageable.

'How's your hangover?' her boss loudly asked Tammy in front of all of her co-workers.

Tammy quit that job not too long after that incident.

Like Tammy, many of us can relate to having been questioned about chronic illness.

I was a few months short of my third birthday when the Chernobyl nuclear disaster occurred. Like countless other people living in Ukraine at the time, my family and I experienced acute radiation poisoning. Many of the side effects of this experience still affect me to this day. Specifically, before it rains and when there are geomagnetic storms in the atmosphere, I experience severe migraines that sometimes lead to seizures.

Although such environmental migraine triggers were well-known in Ukraine, they were not well understood in the United States. For years, I've had U.S. doctors telling me that weather and geomagnetic storms don't cause migraines and that I just need to 'drink more water' and 'focus on stress management'.

And even though I knew that my migraines were always directly tied to environmental factors, I started doubting and gaslighting myself, wondering if I was somehow 'making it up'.

Except that my condition did not improve, and I continued getting worse, as multiple doctors kept telling me that migraines don't cause seizures.

After years of significantly worsening symptoms, I found a doctor who believed me. My neurologist diagnosed me with *hemiplegic migraines*, a rare type of migraine that can cause seizures. I am fortunate enough to have a team of doctors who believe me and support me now, but it took me over twenty years to realise that I can advocate for myself.

I do believe the vast majority of doctors are amazing – the ones who go into medicine for the right reason: to help people.

And still, some providers engage in medical gaslighting – denying or questioning patients' symptoms, making them believe that the root cause of their symptoms is related to something else without proper testing or evidence, and not trusting a patient to self-report the severity of their symptoms.

Some doctors, often without awareness of doing so, are more likely to invalidate the patient's symptoms if the patient is a woman, if they are overweight, or if they are Black.

Historically, Black people were believed to have higher pain tolerance, and were even believed by some to have thicker skin than white patients. Of course, neither of these is the case, and yet to this day, Black people are more likely to endure painful procedures and are more likely to be denied pain medication than white people.[1]

Similarly, sizeism and fat phobia can lead to a lot of people who are overweight being denied proper treatment. One of my clients, 'Mary', went to see her primary-care doctor for a worsening pain in her side. Her doctor didn't offer any tests but told Mary that she needed to lose some weight and referred her to a weight-loss programme. He also suggested that she try exercising and eating better.

'He didn't even ask me if I exercise or what my diet is like,' Mary, a marathon runner, told me. 'I bet he doesn't treat his thin patients the same way. Just once, I want to see a doctor who will treat me *as a person* and focus on my symptoms, and not tie everything to my body size.'

Later that night, Mary went into an emergency room and was admitted for acute appendicitis.

People with both visible and invisible disabilities are frequently unheard after repeated attempts to explain their needs.

1 Strand, et al. (2021)

'My friend invited me to a birthday party at his apartment,' my client 'Carlos' told me. 'I asked if his building was wheelchair accessible. He assured me that it was. But when I showed up, there wasn't a ramp.'

'Oh, I'm so sorry,' I said, 'that's so frustrating. What did you do?'

'I asked my friend about it. He said that he thought that since his building has an elevator, that it meant that it was wheelchair accessible. Except that you have to go up three steps to get into his building before you ever get to the elevator.'

'Jocelyn', a mom of a six-year-old, 'Gloria', shared her story with me.

'Gloria was born with a life-threatening peanut allergy. If she eats peanuts or peanut butter, she gets an anaphylactic reaction – her throat closes, and she can't breathe. If she doesn't get an epinephrine shot at that time, she will die.'

Jocelyn shared that because of her daughter's young age and allergy, Jocelyn monitors every event her daughter attends outside of the house.

'Her school has been wonderful,' Jocelyn said, 'the cafeteria only serves nut-free lunches now. But some of the parents are still packing peanut butter and jelly sandwiches for their children.

'When I asked the parents if they could possibly give their kids nut-free lunches, some of the parents got aggressive. They said, *Why should I change what I pack for my kid just because yours is allergic?* But they don't understand that if their kid smudges peanut butter on the table and Gloria accidentally touches it and then puts her finger in her mouth, like many kids do, she can die. I don't know how to explain to them that they should care about people.'

Jocelyn mentioned that she also must be very careful when flying with her daughter.

'Not every airline is nut-free,' she explained. 'When we fly, the airborne particles from peanuts can cause an allergic reaction because we're in a less ventilated and a more enclosed space. When we board, we have to ask the flight attendants to make an announcement, asking passengers not to eat anything with nuts. Most people are understanding but some are just obnoxious. One time, right after the announcement, the person behind me called her sister and complained loudly that because someone on board has a peanut allergy, she now can't open her candy bar, and that it was unfair. My daughter started crying.'

'What did you do?' I asked her.

'I blew up. I turned around and said, "You know what's unfair? That my daughter will never have a normal childhood. That we have to board early just to wipe down all surfaces of her seat. That she might not be able to have a sleepover until she's a teenager. That we have to vet every restaurant and ask them to cook her meals separately. That the price of epi pens keep surging. But most of all, it's unfair that she'll have to face people like you, who'd rather bitch about some stupid candy bar than realise that by merely not eating it you're saving her life!"'

The examples listed in this chapter are all examples of ableist oppression. People who do not struggle with visible or invisible disabilities are unfortunately more likely to misunderstand and invalidate those who do.

Telling people who struggle with depression, anxiety, trauma or another mental health disorder to 'just think positive' or to 'get over it' are also examples of ableist oppression.

People who are neurodivergent, introverted and/or struggle with anxiety or trauma might understandably feel overwhelmed and overstimulated in loud, crowded or very bright environments. And yet many of us might have been pushed to attend these environments against our wishes by people who fail to understand how difficult and overwhelming these situations might be. Similarly, when people who struggle with frequent suicidal ideation are told that they're doing it 'just to get attention', this too is an example of ableist oppression.

If you've experienced any of these types of oppression, know that you're not alone. You're not 'exaggerating', you're not 'being too sensitive', you're not 'asking for too much'. You're a human being who deserves to be heard. Of course you feel angry and frustrated in these situations! You feel enraged because these situations are enraging.

Because it's your voice vibrating and encouraging you to meet your basic human need – the need to be heard.

Chapter 21
The Fawn Response

'Good morning! Hello! How are you? Are you comfortable? How are you feeling today?' One of my clients, 'Melanie', would say this to me at the start of many of our sessions in the beginning of our work together.

Melanie always wanted to make sure that I was comfortable. And that everyone else around her was taken care of and comfortable as well. Even if it made her very uncomfortable.

Melanie was severely abused as a child. Her way of managing her trauma was to try to make herself as helpful and as useful as she could. As a part of her trauma, Melanie believed that she was emotionally and physically responsible for making other people happy. This meant that if someone was unhappy or uncomfortable in her presence, Melanie would go above and beyond to make them happy. Even if it came at a great personal price. Even if it wasn't what she wanted.

Even if it hurt.

This type of people-pleasing as a way of avoiding conflict with others is called the *fawn response*.

I didn't learn about the fawn response until I was in my mid thirties, despite utilising it since I was a small child. The fawn response might allow us to avoid discomfort in the moment, but it can lead to long-term resentment and anger.

In order for us to better manage the fawn response, we need to understand it. The *fawn response* was first identified by psychotherapist Pete Walker in his brilliant book *Complex PTSD: From Surviving to Thriving.*[1]

The fawn response is a trauma response. It usually comes from a pattern of behaviour we learned in childhood in order to survive and get our needs met. If you grew up in an environment where you were deprived of food, water, affection, company or other basic human needs as a form of punishment, you might have learned people-pleasing behaviours as a way to survive. Or you may have learned fawning behaviour to try to appease your bullies or abusers.

The unfortunate fact is that people-pleasing is a loop that keeps you stuck. It arises from an innocent attempt to be accepted and to belong. However, it doesn't work that way. People-pleasing won't make people like you more. Instead, it will either maintain abusive patterns in your relationships or prevent good people from really getting to know you. People-pleasing won't ensure that you'll be accepted, it only ensures that your needs will remain unmet.

Not expressing your needs or enabling other people's intentional or unintentional mistreatment of you can lead to you feeling disconnected, lonely, angry or frustrated. In some cases, you might take things out on others – usually the closest people to you; the ones you love the most.

Our fawn response can sometimes prevent an uncomfortable

1 Walker (2013)

interaction with one person, but it can also ensure a continuation of unhelpful or even abusive interactions with ourselves and others. Getting stuck in a pattern of constant fawning, and therefore not getting our needs met, can cause panic attacks, migraines and other types of pain, as well as inflammation, mood swings and, in some cases, self-harm or suicidal ideation.

Just like Melanie, I struggled with the fawn response for thirty-five years. One of my husband's friends, let's call him 'Richard', was sometimes abrasive towards my husband and other people in our circle.

'He's just stressed out,' I'd say to my husband after he complained to me about Richard criticising him and making fun of him in public. 'He doesn't mean anything by it.'

I thought I was being understanding. What I was actually doing was gaslighting and invalidating my partner and our friends. And I was letting Richard get away with his behaviours. This is called *enabling*.

Enabling refers to protecting others from being held accountable and from experiencing the full impact of their actions. As a result, the person who is being enabled does not learn that they have to change their behaviours, so they continue them.

I used to think that being a compassionate person meant being understanding. I later learned that there's a big difference between understanding and enabling. We can understand how someone is feeling and what they are going through, and hold them accountable at the same time. My enabling behaviour hurt not only me, it also hurt those closest to me. In trying to 'keep the peace' and walking on eggshells in front of my biggest bullies, I failed to stand up for my partner and others who were hurt.

If there's someone in your life who is harmful to you or others, please know that by setting a boundary, you aren't being mean. You are holding them accountable. And sometimes setting a boundary and being clear with another person about the impact of their actions is the most courageous and also the most compassionate step we can take.

And it's absolutely okay if you don't feel ready. You never have to push yourself beyond your own limits. You don't have to stand up to someone if you don't feel ready yet. Take your time.

In the meantime, see if you can start tracking your fawn response. See if you can silently name it when it's happening or journal about it after the fact.

Here are some questions to consider:

1. Who are the people with whom you're most likely to use the fawn response? Who are you most likely to make excuses for or get defensive on behalf of? Who are you most worried about upsetting? Who do you walk on eggshells around? Who do you most often change plans for? Change your behaviour for? Feel most resentful of?

2. What does your fawn response look like? (For example, do you compliment the other person a lot, smile, hold your breath, avoid talking, or avoid telling them how you feel?)

3. If you knew with 100 per cent certainty that you could be fully honest with the person you're fawning over and that they would understand and be receptive to hearing you out, what would you ideally want to say to them? (It is completely normal to feel anxious and uncomfortable answering this question. If it feels too overwhelming to answer it now, feel free to skip it and come back to it when you're ready.)

4. How does this person's treatment of you make you feel? Do you feel important, included and cared for? Do you feel seen, heard and valued? Do you feel emotionally safe sharing how you feel and what you need?

5. Think of the worst thing this person has done to you. Now, think of someone innocent, like a child, a puppy, a kitten or someone else you'd find both lovable and endearing. Now, imagine the person you fawn over treating that innocent being the way that they treated you. Would you think their behaviour is okay?

Take your time with these reflections. Even if you are not ready to say or do anything different, just observe and reflect – that's already a big step towards self-empowerment.

You are not alone in this. I am in your corner. And so are millions of people who have had the same experiences. We will get through this together. One step at a time.

Chapter 22
To be Heard

I had just started my new job as a postdoctoral trainee. New job meant new health insurance. New health insurance meant a new doctor.

I must have had eight panic attacks in the waiting room. I kept picturing myself over-explaining my chronic illness like I always do, and my doctor not believing me and telling me that I just need to drink more water and try to reduce my stress levels, like they all had.

I walked into the examination room, wringing my cold sweaty hands as a very nice nurse took my vital signs.

'Dr Greene will be right in to see you,' the nurse said with a warm smile and left the room.

Sometime between a minute and an eternity later, Dr Greene walked through the door. She had blonde hair with light green streaks. She had a tiny nose piercing, and I could spot the edge of a tattoo on her wrist, most of it covered by her spotless white coat.

I immediately felt a bit more at ease.

She's different, like me, I thought, touching my own wrist tattoo.

'Hi, I'm Dr Greene,' she smiled at me, 'but feel free to call me Kelly.'

She asked me to tell her a bit about myself and my medical history.

As I talked, she didn't interrupt. She just listened and wrote down some notes.

She was the first doctor that didn't jump in with advice-giving thirty seconds into hearing my symptoms.

I told her about my history of radiation exposure from Chernobyl, my migraines and my seizures.

When I was done speaking, she asked me if there were any specific triggers for my migraines.

'Weather changes,' I said, and braced for an argument. When it didn't come, I carefully added, 'And geomagnetic storms.'

My heart was pounding. I held my breath, waiting for her to tell me that 'that's not how it works'.

But instead, she nodded, wrote it down in her notes and looked up at me. 'This all makes sense, given your history.'

Tears burned my eyes. 'Really? You believe me?'

She gave me a sad smile. 'I gather by your reaction that some of your other doctors didn't. So, let me just say this: not only do I believe you, but I also support you. Modern medicine has many great advantages to it but we're always growing and learning. And when it comes to your body, you are the expert in it.'

She was the best doctor I had ever worked with.

Being heard and validated is sometimes the most healing experience we can have. Being heard creates the opposite experience to loneliness; it creates the experience of connection, and the feelings of soothing, gratitude and validation.

Here are some examples of actions that make us feel heard:

- Being listened to without interruption.
- Being listened to without receiving unsolicited advice.
- Being validated with phrases such as:
  - ◊ 'I believe you'
  - ◊ 'I hear you'
  - ◊ 'That makes sense'
  - ◊ 'I'm so sorry that happened to you'
  - ◊ 'It makes sense you feel this way. I'd feel that way too if I was in this situation'
  - ◊ 'What's the best way I can support you right now?'
  - ◊ 'Thank you for telling me. I appreciate you sharing this with me'
  - ◊ 'I don't even know what to say right now. I'm just glad you felt comfortable enough to tell me'

What are some of the phrases and actions that make you feel heard?

See if you can practise saying them to yourself and, if possible, see if you can ask another person to practise saying them to you.

Dog In the Park

One exercise we can try when feeling unheard or frustrated is the Dog in the Park exercise.

Imagine for a few moments that you are taking your dog to

a dog park (even if you don't actually have a dog). When the dog is on the leash, he's probably excited, hyper, pulling at the leash and difficult (if not impossible) to keep calm. Once you take off the leash, the dog is free to run, play and otherwise express his energy until he feels calm and settled. The best part about a dog park is that the dog is given a great deal of freedom to roam in a safe environment.

Just like taking an actual dog to a dog park to let him run free in a controlled space, we can give our emotions freedom to express themselves in a safe environment.

Many people who are struggling with panic attacks, depression, anxiety or trauma-related feelings experience some of these symptoms:

- Tightness and tension in the neck and shoulders
- Tightness in the chest
- Feeling out of breath
- Heart pounding
- Sweating
- Shaking
- Feeling lightheaded
- Nausea or upset stomach
- Feeling like things are not real (derealisation)
- Flushed cheeks

If you are willing, I'm going to ask you to choose one of the sensations listed above that you experience on a regular basis, starting with the least distressing sensation. Close your eyes and focus only on that sensation. Fully allow it to be present in your body.

Imagine that you can zoom in your attention to only focus on this symptom or sensation now. For example, if you picked 'heart pounding' then focus your entire attention now on just noticing how much your heart is pounding in this moment.

Great! Now, we are going to imagine that the sensation is a dog, and you have just arrived at the dog park, and it's time to take off the leash. That means that just for a few minutes, we are going to only focus on this sensation while allowing it to be here, allowing it to be as strong or as weak as it needs to be.

This means that just for a few minutes, we can really notice your heart pounding in your chest, or your nausea, or your dizziness, or any other sensation that you feel. Set your timer for three minutes (or one minute if three minutes feels too long), and press *START*.

At first, the sensation might get a little worse. This is normal. Breathe.

Focus on your exhale.

Don't try to run away from this feeling. Just focus on *allowing* yourself to feel it. Allow these sensations to be as free as a dog running in a park without a leash.

Ready?

Go!

How did it go?

What did you notice?

Was it tolerable just to focus on this sensation?

Did you notice it getting worse, better or worse again?

Did you notice any other sensations or other thoughts that showed up?

Did you get distracted or wish you could stop or keep checking the timer to see when it would run out?

All of these experiences are okay. They all make sense.

Doing these practices regularly can allow you to make more space for these sensations so that they might feel less overwhelming over time.

Would you be willing to try another one?

See if you can focus on each of these sensations one at a time for at least one minute.

The more we can let our emotions 'off the leash', one element at a time, the easier it can be for us to face these emotions later on.

TAKE AWAYS

- You deserve to be heard.
- Being heard is one of our basic human needs.
- Not being heard feels frustrating and oppressive because it is.
- Sometimes we engage in the fawn (people-pleasing) response to try to get our needs met. In the long-term, the fawn response makes it *less* likely that our needs will be met than if we directly communicate them.
- You're allowed to advocate for yourself and set boundaries with others.
- You can practise soothing yourself with the 5 steps technique and the Dog in the Park technique.

PART 4:
Undervalued

Chapter 23
The Freak, the Outsider and the Never–good–enough

'What are you doing for Christmas?' my classmate 'Liz' asked me on our way to our ninth-grade English class.

I was now fourteen and ever since moving to the United States at the age of twelve, I couldn't figure out the best way to answer this question.

'We're Jewish,' I tried telling Dave, a classmate in seventh grade.

'Oh, so, you celebrate Hanukah?' he asked me.

'Yes,' I tried to explain with the help of my dictionary. 'And we celebrate New Year's.'

'New Year's?' Dave asked. 'You mean you ...' He made sure no one was listening in to our conversation and whispered, '... you drink with the adults.'

'No, no!' I nearly shouted, more from embarrassment than anything. 'We have a New Year's tree. And Santa Claus. We call him Grandfather Frost. And we have presents.'

Dave stared at me for a few moments and then sniggered, 'That's Christmas, silly.'

And since then, I couldn't quite explain it to anyone. How could I?

I couldn't find enough words in English, Russian or Ukrainian to explain what New Year's meant to me.

It was a non-religious holiday in Ukraine, as well as in Russia, and the many nearby countries. And this meant that unlike other holidays, like Christmas or Easter, I didn't feel like an outsider.

On New Year's, the entire country came together as one. People hugged one another and exchanged gifts, carefully placed under the New Year's tree. Everyone toasted at midnight, and kids were allowed to drink sweet fizzy drinks and stay up way past our bedtime. Just the one night of the year. It was the one night that felt magical long after I stopped believing in Grandfather Frost.

'Did you hear me?' Liz asked. 'I said, what are you doing for Christmas?'

I forced a smile and glanced up at her. 'We're Jewish.'

She smiled back. 'Oh, so, Happy Hanukah.'

I swallowed the lump of tears that was building up in my throat and said, 'Thanks.'

Several weeks later, when I got home from a long walk, I found my dad watching TV in the living room.

'Where's Mom?' I asked, standing in front of him.

He waved at me to move out of the way of the TV and replied without looking at me, 'Working late.'

I sat down next to him, 'Papa?'

'Hmm?' he said, still watching the screen.

'It's New Year's Eve. It's our third New Year's Eve without a New Year's tree.'

'We can't afford it,' he said, his gaze still transfixed on the news channel.

I shook his arm. 'Papa? Papa, look at me.'

He sighed and slowly turned toward me but said nothing.

'Look, it's after Christmas,' I pleaded. 'All the Christmas trees, I mean, New Year's trees, are at a discount. Maybe if you have, like, twenty dollars, we can get one?'

To my surprise, my father reached into his wallet and counted his money. 'I have eight dollars and sixty-seven cents.'

'Umm, well, maybe there's one we can find that costs that much?'

My father stared at me for a moment and then sighed. 'Okay, get your coat.'

We walked four blocks through the snow to a nearby pharmacy and walked towards the *Clearance* section.

'They are all over ten dollars,' I said with a frown.

'What about that one?' my dad asked pointing at a foot-and-a-half-tall tree with tiny twinkling lights attached to its branches.

I checked the price tag.

$7.99.

Perfect!

With tax, it came out to $8.63.

I stood at the cash register watching my dad counting the last of his pennies before the cashier handed him the bag with our new tree. He never talked to me much but seeing my dad give everything he had to get me the tree said more than his words ever could.

'Happy New Year,' he said, handing me the tree when we got home.

We took it out of the box and put it on top of the kitchen table.

'It's small,' my dad said, and I could hear the regret in his voice.

'No, no. It's perfect,' I said and plugged in the cord.

The tiny tree lit up with several dozen twinkling lights.

That night, my parents went to bed at ten and I stayed up.

I watched the Times Square New Year's ball drop at midnight.

I imagined watching it with my parents, and sharing desserts and unwrapping presents like we used to.

'Happy New Year,' I said to my imaginary guests at the kitchen table.

'Happy New Year,' I said to the tree.

The tree twinkled but didn't say anything.

'Happy New Year,' I said to my cat, and got ready for bed.

To this day, it doesn't matter if I'm around people from the U.S. or people from Ukraine, or from anywhere else in the world, I still sometimes feel like an outsider. I feel like I don't fit in to either culture, nor with other bicultural people. And although when I am surrounded by people who share my beliefs and core values, I feel a stronger sense of belonging, I still feel like an outsider when I am burned out, stressed out, and when I've been neglecting myself. This does not mean that feeling lonely is a choice. Rather it means that loneliness depends on a variety of factors, including having supportive people in our lives and being able to make time to recharge our energy and heal our internal wounds. None of it happens quickly. Rather, recovering from loneliness is a healing process, which means that it takes time and happens gradually.

For many people, feeling like an outsider is a trauma response.[1] People who experienced trauma, especially abuse, bullying, abandonment, discrimination for their size, skin colour, accent, religious beliefs, disability, financial status, gender identity or sexual orientation, might be living in fear of being excluded and abandoned again, even if surrounded by inclusive and kind people. Therefore, we might feel like an outcast and an outsider as a habit, a kind of a self-protective reaction, which can lead to the belief that we do not have intrinsic value. I refer to this as feeling undervalued.

In addition, if you are outspoken about mental health, human rights, advocacy, history, technology or fandom you might struggle feeling connected to people who talk about more superficial topics or issues that you find hurtful and offensive. And the lonelier we feel, the less motivated we might feel to form meaningful connections with others. Luckily, the opposite is true, too – when we start forming meaningful connections with others, our desire to continue doing so increases.[2] This means that the most challenging part is just taking that one first step.

It also means that if you are feeling lonely, as if you don't fit in with others because you feel that you are too different from them, there's nothing wrong with you. You could be experiencing a trauma reaction, you could be burned out, or you could be spending time with people who don't share your core values.

1 Lin & Chiao (2020); Murthy (2020)
2 Murthy (2020)

One of the people I interviewed for this book, 'Lisa', shared with me that when her parents divorced, she felt like an outsider. She reported that it felt as if she had a terrible flaw that she wanted to keep secret but that everyone knew about.

'I felt like I had a mark on me,' she told me. 'I had to be "perfect". I couldn't drink, I couldn't party, I couldn't date, or people would say that I was acting out because I came from a *broken home.*'

Lisa also said that she felt like she always had to be the fixer and organiser. She would volunteer to be in charge of events but never a part of them because she didn't feel like she belonged. Like Lisa, many of us were made to feel that we don't belong, that society was judging us for circumstances we had no control over (just as Lisa had no control over her parents' divorce). We may have also been excluded or bullied by others as a result.

If this has happened to you, if you've ever been mistreated for your parents' divorce or your own, for having a disability, a stutter, or for your size, sexual orientation, race, gender identity, socioeconomic status, or for any other reason, please know that it was never about you. You were mistreated because the other person (or people) made a choice to abuse you, and not because you ever did anything to deserve being treated that way.

That thing that others made you feel bad about – that thing about you that you always try to hide – it doesn't make you unlovable. On the contrary. It is one of the most lovable things about you. Yes, THAT ONE.

You have the knowledge and the experience to help others in your same situation. And so, rather than trying to hide one of your loveliest qualities to impress someone whom it's not your job to impress, what if you were unapologetically yourself? What if your experience will lead you to find your own group of people who feel the same way you do and already want exactly what you have to offer? What if you were able to show off, with pride, the things that make you *you*?

Together, we are going to look at some patterns that can contribute to you feeling undervalued. We are also going to look for ways to heal from your painful experiences and create a sense of belonging with yourself and others.

Chapter 24
Binary Thinking

Many of us fall into the trap of binary thinking, also known as 'all-or-nothing' thinking. When we engage in binary thinking, we might think in absolutes. For example, we might think, 'If I'm not perfect, then I'm a failure' or, 'If I'm different, then there's something wrong with me', assuming that there's *a right way* and *a wrong way* to be.

Binary thinking is rigid and inflexible, and as a result, it stifles our creativity and also our individuality. It makes us believe that unless we fall into some kind of a strict category, then there's something wrong with us.

We can get even more stuck in binary thinking when we compare ourselves to others. For example, if you are feeling depressed and lonely in a group of people, where everyone else seems to be cheerful, you might assume that there's something wrong with you. You might engage in binary thinking that it's good to be cheerful, and that it's bad to feel depressed. You might also compare your perceived flaws to other people's greatest accomplishments as a way to shame yourself, feeling even lonelier as a result. This is called the *iceberg effect*.

When we see an iceberg in the water, we typically see only its tip. The majority of the iceberg is submerged under water. That means that what we usually see from other people – their successes and joys – is just the tip of who they are and merely a small fraction of their experience. What we don't see are the setbacks, the adversity, their struggle with imposter syndrome and feeling 'not good enough', as well as feelings of anxiety, worthlessness and loneliness.

Some of the people you admire and look up to the most have the exact same fears, insecurities and struggles as you do. And more so, some of the people you know might be wishing that they were as calm or as talented as you. They too might be seeing only the tip of your iceberg while not seeing your struggles and adversities.

Whenever I bring up this idea to my clients, they initially dismiss it. 'That's ridiculous. That other person is so confident and popular. They are happy and successful, and people naturally like them. And me, I just feel awkward all the time, like I just don't fit in anywhere.'

As a naturally awkward person myself, I actually find awkward people endearing, authentic and likeable. In fact, I would much rather talk to someone who is honest, authentic and awkward than someone who is gregarious, gaudy and over-confident.

Furthermore, if you are a deep-thinking person, you might despise small talk. As a result, your feelings of not fitting in might actually be an indication of boredom. I often tell people that I am *allergic to small talk*. As an empath and an introvert, I value conversations with emotional depth and get worn out by surface-level conversations. If, like me, you are someone who values compelling conversations and emotional depth, you might feel bored by surface-level conversations, but mistakenly believe that there's something wrong with you if you're not enjoying them.

If you ever feel like you don't fit in, if you feel lonely in a crowd or lonely by yourself, if you feel like people don't understand you, then perhaps the problem isn't you. Perhaps what's actually happening is that you are ready to be open and authentic, to talk about issues that matter to you, and perhaps the people in your circle aren't.

It takes a lot of courage to be authentic and not everyone has the courage that you do. Many prefer to hide behind metaphorical masks, pretending that they are 'fine' when they are far from it. Others might be just like you, feeling that they don't belong and wishing that they had someone to relate to, not realising that you feel the same way.

And if this was the case, and you knew with 100 per cent certainty that someone in your circle felt the exact same way as you, how would that change how you interact with them? What might you stand to gain? What if someone else needs to hear exactly what you have to say because they feel it too but are too afraid to express it? What if your truth can bring hope and healing to others?

You have the power and ability to help and inspire other people. You have the gift that other people need. You *are* the gift.

Chapter 25
Virgin Martinis

I always hated the smell of alcohol. And at six years old, when I took a big gulp of vodka, thinking that it was a bottle of cold water on a hot sunny day, I hated the taste of it, too. The smell reminded me of my dad on one of his 'bad days', and the taste of it burned my mouth and made my eyes water.

I managed to get through high school and college without drinking. As an empath and a highly sensitive person, I never liked the loud, overstimulating setting of a bar, and usually hung out in quiet coffee shops with a couple of friends.

However, when I moved from New York to California to start a clinical psychology programme, I suddenly found myself not fitting in with my new friends because I was sober. Since I've always felt like an outsider in different ways, I just added not drinking to the list of what made me different. My friends and I would study and hang out together. Them having alcohol around me never bothered me.

One Saturday evening, I reached out to our friend group to see if anyone was interested in getting together for a game night. All of them said they had plans. I thought nothing of it until I saw pictures of all of them in a bar, on social media.

I was stunned and sincerely hurt. It felt like a deliberate exclusion.

I called one of my friends the next day to ask about it. My friend deeply apologised and said that she didn't think I would have any interest in going to a bar and didn't want to make me feel uncomfortable by inviting me.

'I'm so sorry you felt excluded,' she said. 'We were just trying to be considerate of your needs. Now that I know you don't mind, we'll invite you for sure.'

Phew, I thought. *I'm just making a big deal over nothing.*

But two weeks later it happened again.

And then again.

And again.

In two years, my friends invited me out to a bar with them a total of two times. I would enjoy a virgin martini and my time with them. But a few weeks later, they would again go out to the bar and leave me out.

For the longest time, I thought that there was something wrong with me and wondered why they kept leaving me out of going to the bar but would invite me to go to museums, cafés or to study together.

My trauma narrative (a story that I formed in my mind because of my trauma) told me that I was *unlovable*, and that my friends simply tolerated my company.

It wasn't until years later that one of them admitted to what was happening.

'We *did* exclude you,' he said to me, lowering his head. 'It was intentional but it's not what you think. It wasn't that we didn't want to be around you. It was that we didn't want you to see us drunk.'

'Why?' I asked, both relieved and confused at the same time.

He looked up at me. 'Because it's embarrassing. We thought you'd judge us.'

'I'd never—' I tried protesting.

But my friend shook his head. 'It's not real, I know that. It's not rational. It's just how it felt. Anyway, you deserve to know the truth and I'm sorry.'

I was truly stunned. I spent my entire life thinking that if people excluded me, it was because they didn't want to be around me, that they were judging me and punishing me with rejection. It hadn't occurred to me that people might exclude me because they were afraid of *me judging them*. This experience gave me a lot of perspective about why some people pull away, highlighting the fact that many of us share the same fears – the fears of being judged and rejected.

We spend most of our free time worrying about what other people think of us. We go through our recent and ancient interactions, groaning from embarrassment about something we might have said or done in the past, or worrying about what people will think of us in the future. This can lead to feelings of loneliness and shame.

What you might not realise is that pretty much everyone you know also worries about being judged or rejected by you. Most people you know also groan at remembering embarrassing things they've done and worry about what you and other people might be thinking of them.

People who stop drinking often worry about what others will think about them being sober, not realising that their friends might worry about being judged for continuing to drink. People who spend a lot of time studying in school might fear being judged by those who spend more time partying, not realising that the students who party fear being judged for not studying enough.

And so, what if you went into every situation with the assumption that everyone around you fears being judged? How might that make you feel about other people? How would you show up then?

Chapter 26
Imposter Syndrome

After I'd completed my Ph.D. in behavioural neuroscience, I was invited to teach a psychopharmacology course, in which clinical psychology students would learn about how different psychiatric medications affect people's mental and physical health.

The university director personally asked me to teach this course given my research background and given that I had taught psychology courses for four years prior to that time. However, as it was my first time teaching doctorate-level students and my first time teaching in California after having moved there from New York, my imposter syndrome skyrocketed.

Have you ever felt like you're not good enough? Like you don't actually deserve the responsibility, award or recognition you received? Have you ever felt like you're an imposter, and if someone really got to know you, or your art or your story, they would reject you?

In my case, I was convinced that the university should have hired another instructor, that I was the wrong person for the job, and that the students and other faculty would surely realise it and that I would get fired.

None of that happened.

But that didn't stop me from having massive panic attacks

all semester as I was preparing my lesson plans. I knew about imposter syndrome, but I was convinced that in my situation, my fears of imposterism were actually true.

Scientists estimate that 70 per cent of people[1] struggle with *imposter syndrome*,[2] the belief that you're an imposter and that soon enough everyone will find out and you will be rejected, fired or publicly shamed.

Although people attribute these worries to imposter syndrome, the term *syndrome* isn't exactly accurate. This is not a psychiatric disorder but rather a very common experience.

Imposter syndrome affects people of all disciplines – from doctors to scientists, to college students, to teachers, to writers, artists, musicians, athletes, parents, social media influencers and many others.

Having imposter syndrome does not mean that you are not good enough or that you do not deserve the support, recognition or achievements that you received. Rather, it means that you care. It means that you care so much about the current situation and the people involved that you want to make sure you do a good job. And that means you're the perfect person for this role and this opportunity. This feeling of being 'not good enough', of being an imposter, it doesn't mean that you don't belong. Rather, it means you're exactly where you're supposed to be.

For more information on managing imposter syndrome, check out an amazing book by Jill Stoddard, *Imposter No More*.[3]

1 Sakulku & Alexander (2011)
2 Clance & Imes (1978)
3 Stoddard (2023)

Many people automatically assume that if they think that they are 'not good enough', then it must be true and that they must wait until they feel good enough to live their life the way they want to. For example, some people might wait to date, apply for a job, ask for a promotion or work on their biggest creative passion until they feel 'good enough' and 'ready'. We might also erroneously believe that everyone else already feels good enough and knows exactly what they are doing.

The problem with these assumptions is that they leave us discouraged and prone to inaction, in a constant state of waiting. Rather than putting our lives on hold, researchers suggest that the best way to manage imposter syndrome is to talk about it.[4] Since most people feel this way at least at some point in their lives, and many people feel this way most of the time, conversations about these experiences can be a relief not only for you, but also for the other person. Finding commonality about this shared experience can normalise it and reduce the shame that we feel about it.

Another advantage of talking about your imposter syndrome is to notice that for most people it serves as a representation of what we care about the most. In fact, I find that the inverse of our greatest fears points to our greatest core values. For example, if you worry about not being good enough in your job or school, it is because you care about integrity and honour. If you fear being rejected by others, it is likely because you care about connection and belonging.

4 Clance & Imes (1978); Stoddard (2023)

I'd like to invite you to try out the following exercise:

1. Write out some of your 'not good enough' thoughts, for example, 'I'm not a good enough teacher', 'I'm not a smart enough student', 'I'm not a good enough parent' or 'I'm not a good enough partner'.

2. Change the negative words, such as 'not good enough' to 'I care'. For example, 'I'm not a good enough teacher' becomes 'I care about my students' or 'I care about learning'; 'I'm not a good enough parent' becomes 'I care about my kids'.

3. Write out 1-2 actions you'd like to take in the near future to honour the values you identified in step two, for example, 'I am going to work on a new lesson plan for twenty minutes' or 'I'm going to plan a fun activity for my family'.

See if you can practise these steps over the next few weeks to honour your values. And remember, if you struggle with thoughts of not being good enough, it is because you care, otherwise you wouldn't worry about it. You are good enough even if your anxiety is telling you otherwise. You are good enough precisely because you care so deeply.

Chapter 27
Slots and Vending Machines

I have always felt like an outsider, but never more than when, at twelve, I first moved to the United States from Ukraine.

Two of my classmates, 'Anna' and 'Christina', were from Europe and understood some Ukrainian.

I was thrilled to have someone to talk to, even if we needed to use dictionaries to communicate.

However, Anna and Christina made it very clear that they were open to being friendly, but they were already best friends, and were not looking to add another friend to their group.

Of course, I was hurt, but I appreciated their honesty.

A few weeks after that conversation, Anna approached me after school.

'Hey,' she said, 'do you want to walk home together? It's in the same direction.'

I turned around to make sure she was talking to me. There was only a wall behind me.

'I'm talking to you, silly,' she giggled.

'But what about . . .' I looked from side to side to make sure no one could hear us and whispered, 'Christina?'

Anna didn't seem concerned with keeping her voice down. 'Christina and I aren't friends any more. She's a bitch.'

I gasped, both from surprise and from the curse-word. 'What happened?'

Anna rolled her eyes. 'She talks about people behind their backs. And she's just mean.'

She turned to walk towards the school exit. 'Are you coming?'

'Oh, um, yes, of course,' I said, running after her and trying to process what just happened.

Over the next week, we sat together at lunch, walked home together, and talked on the phone every day.

'We're best friends, aren't we?' Anna asked me one Friday afternoon as we were walking home for the fifth time.

I grinned at her. 'Of course.'

On Monday, I saw Anna and Christina walking arm in arm again like they did before their big fight.

I walked up to them, my stomach dropping. I forced a smile. 'I'm so glad you two made up.'

'Don't,' Christina said. 'Anna told me what you said about me.'

I choked on my breath. 'I didn't—'

'There's no need to lie to my best friend,' Anna said to me. 'Just stay away from us.'

They walked away and I was left alone with my thoughts.

Did this really just happen?

Several weeks later, Anna approached me again. 'Look, I'm sorry about before. It wasn't fair to you. You are such a great friend. I see that now. And Christina, she was wrong about you. And wrong to talk to you that way.'

I was stunned. Her kindness was something I craved but never expected. 'What about Christina?'

Anna waved her arm as if waving away an annoying mosquito. 'Forget her. We don't need her. We can be each other's best friend.'

Over the next six months, Anna and I were 'on again, off again' best friends. Usually, our friendship would last one to two weeks before she and Christina would make up and ditch me again.

And although, over time, I grew less and less surprised by Anna's behaviour, I *was* surprised by mine.

I realised what she was doing, but I kept on giving her one chance after another. She knew just the right things to say to pull me back in. She was charming and charismatic, while I was lonely and desperate.

When she would call, I would drop all my plans so I could hang out with her, without thinking of the consequences of my actions.

During one of our 'on again' friendship phases, Anna pulled me aside. 'Oh my gosh! I saw Christina's mom walking her to school this morning. Can you believe it? It's like she needs her *mommy* to walk her to school.'

'Right,' I said, unsure of what I was supposed to say but not arguing.

'I gotta go. Meet me after school,' she said and ran off.

When I stepped outside onto the chilly, rainy street at the end of the school day, and looked for Anna among the sea of umbrellas, my heart stopped.

My mom stood by the school gate, holding her large, blue umbrella. She waved at me. *Great! Just what I need! For Anna to see my mommy picking me up.*

I ran over to my mom, hunching my shoulders and trying to make myself as small as possible.

'Ma! What are you doing here?' I hissed at her.

My mom raised her eyebrows. 'What do you mean? I brought you an umbrella.'

I looked around from side to side. No sign of Anna yet. *Phew!*

I glared at my mom. 'You have to leave. Someone can see you.'

My mom blanched. Her lip quivered.

But only for a moment.

Her stoic facial expression – her usual one – was back as if it never left.

'Fine,' she said and shoved the blue umbrella into my hands. 'But take this, so you don't get sick.'

With that, she turned around and quietly walked away, soaking in the pouring rain.

I think back to that moment often. I hurt my mom in my desperate attempts to be valued by Anna, but the truth is Anna never valued me. In my attempts to be valued by her I failed to value myself and those around me.

Over the years that I've been working with clients, I've seen many people – kids, adolescents and adults alike – fall into the same pattern of chasing someone who does not value them. Whether this pattern is with a friend, a significant other or a family member, many of us might lose ourselves in trying to find a semblance of a connection with that person.

To help my clients understand what I wish I'd known back then, I use the slots versus vending machines metaphor.

Vending machines (usually) give you what you paid for. It's a fair exchange. The money you put in is equal to what you get in return, in terms of value.

On the other hand, if you put a dollar in a slot machine, you could get ten dollars, you could get hundreds of dollars, or you could get nothing. Most often, you get nothing.

The unpredictability of the slot machine can be exciting – all those blinking lights and money pouring out if you win – but more often than not, you have to put in a lot of your resources (dollars) and get nothing in return.

Over time, you can become addicted to rush and excitement. Even if you usually lose, you might get so obsessed with the possibility of winning that you lose yourself in the process and hurt those closest to you by either ignoring their needs or using up all your time and resources on chasing this addiction.

Think about a relationship you've had where you feel like you are walking on eggshells, too afraid to speak your truth.

Ask yourself, *Is this a vending machine relationship or a slot machine relationship? Is it healthy?* Does this person meet your needs? Do they even try?

Are you getting hurt because of this relationship? Are other people in your life getting hurt because of this relationship?

Depending on the answers to these questions, it might be time to re-evaluate this relationship, especially if the other person doesn't regularly meet your needs or harms you in some way.

Because you deserve better. You deserve to feel valued, to know where you stand, and to be treated with kindness and respect.

Chapter 28
Shame Spiral

It wasn't until I was halfway done with my presentation that I realised, to my horror, *I was presenting the wrong presentation to the wrong audience.*

Instead of giving a lecture on suicide prevention to a group of veterans, the lecture I was actually hired to do, I was in the middle of presenting a lecture targeted towards mental health professionals who treat veterans.

It was something I couldn't even have imagined in my worst anxiety-driven nightmares.

'It was an honest mistake,' my partner tried to reassure me after I was done with the lecture. 'It could have happened to anyone. Besides, you recovered halfway through and focused on the veterans.'

But none of it mattered. Not to me.

I called and emailed the event organiser, apologising and insisting she not pay me. She was kind and told me not to worry about it. But none of that mattered to my internal shame monster.

You're such an idiot! my shame monster screamed inside my head. *You've got to be the biggest moron alive! These people counted on you, and you let them down. Who does that?*

I imagined all the attendees and the organisers saying how terrible my presentation was.

I followed up with the event organiser again and offered to teach another webinar free of charge, but the shame monster wasn't appeased, especially when I did not hear back from the organiser.

Idiot! You're so stupid; you don't deserve to be hired again. Even free of charge.

You don't deserve to live.

Violent images flooded my mind of how I should punish myself. Although I didn't act on any of the thoughts, I felt sick to my stomach. After a frenzied hour of desperately trying to fix my mistake, I shut down and must have stared at the tiny cracks in the wall paint for the next two hours.

Shame spiral.

That's what I was going through. Although I have spent years helping my clients manage their shame spiral, I was metaphorically knocked off my feet when it happened to me.

In over a decade of my work with trauma survivors, I observed the shame spiral manifest as a series of predictable steps:

1. **Shock and frenzy**: either desperately trying to fix the situation or obsessively reviewing it in your mind.
2. **Beliefs that others are judging you** as harshly as you judge yourself.
3. **Anger:** starting with self-debasement or self-abuse, this sometimes turns into blaming others or extreme defensiveness.
4. **Nausea or headache** or another body reaction.

5. **Shutting down and numbing out**: this may be by not speaking or moving, using substances, overeating, watching TV, scrolling on social media or playing video games. I want to be very clear – there is absolutely nothing wrong with eating delicious foods, enjoying a TV show or playing a fun video game. It's when we use them to avoid emotions that they can become problematic. Other shutting-down or numbing behaviours could include self-harm, aggressive driving, yelling or starting fights.

6. **Feeling further ashamed** for the way we reacted in step five and emotionally beating ourselves up, starting the cycle all over again.

7. **Further avoidance** of talking about the situation we're ashamed of. In fact, when I first started drafting this chapter, the thought of writing about giving the wrong lecture gave me a headache. I seriously considered writing about a less embarrassing moment of my life, but it would have been neither honest nor authentic within the topic of this chapter.

Most of us cycle through the steps of the shame spiral several times (although not always in the same order). The pattern sometimes becomes worse after a while, in some cases turning into depression, panic attacks, social anxiety disorder, chronic pain or addiction. However, it can become better if we can understand why it's happening and learn to engage with our shame spiral differently.

In order to change how we respond to the shame spiral we need to first understand why we feel shame in the first place. Self-compassion researcher Chris Germer once said that 'shame is an innocent emotion that arises from the wish to be loved'[1]. According to Brené Brown, a researcher who studies vulnerability and shame, shame is a universal emotion, meaning that we all experience it. And the less we talk about shame, the more we feel it.[2]

Because of our terror of rejection and abandonment, we tend to isolate when we feel shame, sometimes pushing people away. This is why shame is such a lonely experience – it becomes a combination of self-abuse and isolation.

In addition to fearing social rejection, another reason we might get trapped in the shame spiral is when we do something that violates our moral code. Me delivering the wrong presentation to the veteran community was in direct violation of my moral code to try to help people. When we do something that goes against our moral code, we can experience something called *moral injury*.[3] Moral injury usually presents with shame and, in some cases, can lead to PTSD.

The final reason why some of us might experience shame is due to trauma.[4] Those of us who have been abused, bullied, abandoned or persecuted against might experience shame as a trauma response. When we have been abused, we might

1 Germer (2019)
2 Brown (2015)
3 Vermetten & Jetly (2018)
4 Platt & Freyd (2012)

internalise our abuser's voice as our own and beat ourselves up so that others don't have to.

Taking some time to reflect on the origins of our shame responses can help us to better understand them.

What are some of your own origins of your shame responses? Is it the fear of rejection and abandonment, or the concern of not acting within your moral code, or is it a trauma response? In many situations, the origins include all of the above.

MANAGING A SHAME SPIRAL

When you're caught in a shame spiral, try the following seven steps, some of which we've already practised:

1. **Name it:** Remind yourself, 'This is a shame spiral. I've been through this before.'
2. **Feel it and stretch into it:** Notice where in your body you feel it most. Many people experience shame in their stomach, as well as chest, throat and jaw. Notice where you're holding shame in your body.
3. **Breathe into it:** When in a shame spiral, we need to take longer intervals to breathe into our body than usual.

   - Set your timer for three minutes (or count twenty breaths if you don't have a timer).
   - Breathe in deeply, and with each exhale, focus on unwinding and loosening the specific area of your body where you feel shame. Focus on the exhale.

- If you feel shame in more than one area of your body, it's helpful to practise a separate set of three-minute breathing intervals for each body part.

4. **Vent:** Vent to a trusted friend, a diary or a pillow. Using your words and letting out how you feel can help to soothe some of the shame feelings in our body.

5. **Move:** It might seem strange but moving is one of the most helpful things we can do to offset shame. When we experience shame, our body goes into a *freeze* response. As a result, we might slouch, make ourselves smaller, and barely move. You might notice that your body wants to collapse at the midpoint, as if to have you fold yourself in half at the stomach. Let it. Collapse your body and fold it even further and then, one vertebra at a time, sit up or stand up, stretching your body as wide as possible, and then try to move around.

   By moving – walking around, going for a run, doing a few jumping jacks, or even doing ten air push-ups – you can help to shift your body from the shame-induced *freeze* response to a more active and empowered state, where you can make good decisions.[5]

6. **Review your core values:** Our biggest fears and our deepest shame reactions point to the foundation of our most deeply held core values. This means that we can analyse our anxiety and shame reactions as a compass

5 Levine (2010)

to point to what we care about most. For example, if you feel guilty over saying something unkind in an argument and are shaming yourself by telling yourself that you're 'a terrible person', this is an indication that you value kindness.

In my example, when I presented the wrong lecture, I shamed myself by saying that *I'm an idiot* and that *other people were counting on me, and I let them down.* In this case, my affected core values were those of integrity and helping people.

7. **Take a step to honour your core values:** Once you recognise what your core values are, think of one possible step you can take to honour your core values. Ask yourself, *Is there any way to remedy the situation, by apologising or otherwise?* If not, or if you've already tried and are still stuck in a shame spiral, ask yourself, *What can I do differently in the future?* Write down your plan.

Repeat these steps as necessary. Remember that you are a good person. Bad people don't worry about whether they've done something wrong, they just do it. You're a good person and you deserve to be treated with kindness and dignity, even by yourself.

Especially by yourself.

Chapter 29
Parentified

I was raised to be 'a good girl'. This meant taking care of my parents' and my brother's emotions, keeping the family secrets, and not being 'a nuisance'.

When one of the members of my family would hit me, I would tell myself, 'I must have deserved it.' I believed that if I got better at understanding their moods and 'not bothering them when they are stressed', then I wouldn't be punished. I didn't know then that this belief is called the *illusion of control*.[1]

I thought that if I was more vigilant about my family's stress levels and worked harder to make them happy, I wouldn't get hurt. I thought I was in control, but this was a story that my mind created in order to keep me safe because I was in no place to face the truth.

Some of us have been abused and parentified as children. *Parentified* means that we had to act like an adult and take care of our caretakers' emotional needs. When we are expected to act like a parent while we are still a child, our own emotional needs aren't met. If you were expected to take care of your parents' emotional, material or physical needs rather than being allowed to be a child, you were parentified. And parentification

1 Jones & Barlow (1990)

is a type of child abuse, often as a combination of emotional or physical abuse and emotional neglect.

As human beings who are wired for connection, our neural programming wants us to reach out for support when we are suffering. This is why babies cry and why toddlers reach out their tiny arms to their caregivers – to be held. In every sense of that word.

But once we become teenagers and adults, most of us are not only discouraged but also deeply shamed or even punished for attempting to communicate our emotional needs.

When we are parentified, rather than being allowed to cry or to ask our caregivers to meet our needs, we take on the responsibility of meeting theirs. Worse, in some instances, we might be made to feel that our very survival depends on being able to meet our caregivers' needs. This is parentification. This is child abuse.

Whether we're going through a break-up, a fight with a close friend, trying to find our sense of identity or struggling with chronic illness (including chronic pain, autoimmune disease, chronic depression, persistent anxiety, etc.), some people in our life will not understand. They will invalidate our experience, telling us, 'Other people have it worse.' They will tell us that 'at least it wasn't as bad as it could have been'. These are all harmful and invalidating responses, although in some cases they occur out of a genuine desire to help but a lack of understanding of how to do so.

In other cases, people might tell you to 'stop whining', to 'grow up' or that 'your uncle has cancer, he has it so much worse'.

By invalidating your experiences, the people in your life are basically saying, 'Your suffering is of no concern to me. You should suffer in silence or suppress your feelings. I do not wish to help you and if you keep trying to get my help, I will punish you.'

As a result, we suffer twice – once from the initial situation and then from the shame and rejection of others. We might feel alone in our circumstances and lonely in our processing of them. And because of this, we might be forced to grow up too quickly, to be more independent than we were ready for, to be shamed for needing others in our time of suffering.

Throughout my childhood, my mom would get very angry with me if I ever told her that I was feeling depressed. She would shame me for being 'ungrateful' for what I had and would yell at me until I would apologise.

When I was in graduate school, I called her one day, crying. I said that I was really struggling with depression and had a difficult time coping.

She took a big breath before responding in a very terse tone. 'Listen to me. I need you to understand once and for all that you may never EVER come to me with things like this. You're not the only one struggling.'

And then she hung up.

Our dynamic changed forever that day. I have never again reached out to her when I was struggling. And it was also the first time that I was able to reflect on how parentified I was. I started reflecting that most of the time when I would try to talk to my mother about my emotional struggles, she would shame me, invalidate me or create a situation that was focused on her.

I was hurt, sure, but the clarity of it helped me to find peace. I realised that I was never the daughter, nor the baby sister. I was always 'the container', the healer, the mother.

And now I get to choose how often we talk and the boundaries I set. I also no longer expect them to play the part of my parents because I can accept that they aren't capable of that. Being the parent was always my role until I was able to find members of my *chosen family* – a kind of family we make by choice.

Not all the relationships we have are healthy for us, even with our closest family members. Take some time and reflect on the most significant relationships of your life. Were any of them hurtful? Of those that were particularly hurtful, were you being abused and/or parentified? Were you expected to be a parent or an adult while you were still a child? Were your own needs neglected?

If you were parentified or abused, know that it isn't your fault. People who tend to hurt us the most are often the ones that see a reflection of their own shadow through the love of our hearts. Because of your kindness, because of your sweet and gentle nature, some people might notice how unkind and hurtful they have been. And sometimes the shame of that experience makes them lash out even more. It's not okay. None of it was okay.

You deserve better. You always have.

I see you. I see your pain. I value you.

You matter more than you can possibly imagine.

Chapter 30
It's Not You, It's Management

'I appreciate what you're saying, Doc, but there just aren't enough hours in the day,' my client, 'Luke', said to me.

'Not enough hours to do what?' I enquired.

'Any of it,' Luke said. 'Any of this self-care stuff you're talking about. A walk. Meditation. A few minutes to myself. On most days, I don't even have time to go to the bathroom. On the rare occasions that I eat at work, I eat at my desk while muting myself during phone meetings.'

When I asked Luke to describe his typical week to me, he said, 'I get up at four forty five a.m. I work at home from five to six thirty a.m. Then, I help my wife with the kids and then drive to work. I get to work around seven thirty or eight a.m.

'I'm in meetings all day. Everything is late. Everything is urgent. I work until seven p.m. Then I rush home. Help my wife with the kids at bedtime. Then I eat, sometimes for the first time that day. Then I work until eleven or midnight and collapse. On weekends, I sleep in until seven a.m. and usually work from home until eight p.m. or later. I only get paid for forty hours per week and my company doesn't pay overtime. On most weeks, I put about eighty-five to ninety hours into my job. And it's not enough. I feel like no matter what I do, it's never enough. I tried bringing it up to my manager, but his response to everything is, "You're just going to have to figure it out.'"

Like Luke, many of us have experienced the toxic work culture that places deadlines and achievement over the person. There might be shaming, workplace bullying and failing to see, hear and value employees – by treating them as cogs in the machine instead of as human beings. Many employees get severely burned out. Burnout is not only exhaustion – people experiencing burnout often feel depressed, irritable, anxious or might struggle with headaches, stomach ulcers, insomnia or panic attacks. In severe cases, burnout can lead to stroke, heart attack or premature death.[1]

In October 2022, the United States Surgeon General, Dr Vivek Murthy, released a special report outlining the impacts of toxic workspaces on our physical and mental health. In his report, he also outlined the *Five Essentials for Workplace Mental Health and Well-Being*. These include protection from harm (creating environments that are both physically and psychologically safe for employees and normalise and support mental health), connection and community (fostering a culture of inclusion and belonging and a focus on collaboration and teamwork), work–life harmony (creating flexible schedules and adequate time off, as well as a clear boundary between work and non-work time), mattering at work (valuing employees' decisions and offering gratitude and recognition for their work) and opportunities for growth (offering quality training,

1 Ahola, et al. (2010); Melamed, et al. (2006)

as well as clear and helpful feedback, and pathways for career advancement).[2]

Luke's job seemingly failed to address his needs in all five categories.

'I tried taking a leave of absence from work last year,' Luke told me. 'My blood pressure was sky high, and my doctor insisted I take time off.'

'How did it go?' I asked.

'The rest was nice but when I got back, things got piled up. To make it worse, my manager started treating me differently. Now, every time he puts me on a new project, he asks me, "So, do you think you can handle this one or is it going to *stress you out?*" He actually used his fingers to do the air quotes and his tone was very passive-aggressive. Some of my co-workers overheard it and made snide remarks later. It was humiliating.'

Like Luke, some people find themselves in a toxic work environment, experiencing workplace bullying, harassment, microaggressions, humiliation and discrimination. Of course, such practices are unethical and illegal, but that doesn't mean that they don't occur.

We might engage in self-gaslighting by telling ourselves that we're just imagining that our work conditions are that extreme, or we might fake being 'well enough' because of fear of being demoted or losing our jobs.

In some cases, we get so caught up in the insurmountable amount of work and pressure placed on us that we don't have

2 Murthy (2022)

time to step back and realise that we are in an abusive relationship with our management. For many of us, stress, survival and overwork become our safety zone.

A lonely, terrifying safety zone.

And even when we realise it, stepping out of this pattern can seem both terrifying and impossible.

'I have a wife and two small children to take care of,' Luke told me. 'I have a mortgage to pay. Bills. I can't quit now. I keep telling myself that I just gotta hang on for another twelve years. When we pay off our mortgage and my kids are off to college, I can walk into my manager's office, give him the middle finger and resign on the spot.'

'I hear that,' I said, 'and I see how important it is to you to be able to take care of your family. And also, what if you could do that but didn't have to work ninety-hour weeks for the next twelve years? Would it be okay if we examine some options?'

Luke shifted in his seat. 'I don't know. I have a lot riding on this. I don't want to ruffle any feathers. What will happen to my family if I leave this job?'

'What will happen to your family if you don't?' I asked.

He swallowed and nodded. Over the next few months, Luke started taking seemingly small steps - steps that led to big changes.

It started with him not working Sundays. This wasn't easy and there were some Sundays during which Luke still put in two to three hours of work, but for the most part he focused on resting and spending time with his family.

'How do you feel?' I asked Luke a month after he started taking Sundays off.

'A little bit more rested,' he said, 'but definitely still burned out and exhausted. I feel like it will take a year to recover from nearly ten years of this schedule.' He looked up at me. 'And I also realised something.'

'What's that?' I asked him.

'I realised that I will never meet the deadlines.' He shook his head. 'It's so wild, you know? I've been at this job for almost ten years, and this entire time I've been hustling to meet their deadlines. But all of us are so overworked, understaffed and burned out that we can't possibly meet the management's deadlines. We'll always be behind schedule until THEY hire more people. And once I realised that, I stopped rushing. Don't get me wrong, I still work my butt off every day. But I took the pressure off myself to meet the deadlines and instead, I'm just focusing on what I *can* do.'

Over the next few months, Luke started *quiet quitting* – a term that has come to mean putting in the necessary amount of work but not extra. It also refers to setting better boundaries at work rather than following the hustle–burnout work culture. Examples of quiet quitting include not checking work phone or emails after 5 p.m. or on weekends, taking a vacation, and not volunteering for additional projects when your plate is already full.

After Luke and I talked about quiet quitting, he started setting firmer boundaries with himself about how early he started working and how late he stopped. He turned off his laptop at 8 p.m. and didn't check his phone until the following morning. He stopped bringing his work phone when he went out with his family. Several months later, Luke started interviewing for other jobs.

'I don't want to just take the first job that's offered to me,' he told me. 'As they are interviewing me, I'm interviewing them, too. One of the first questions I now ask at interviews is about their work–life balance.'

It took Luke six months of interviewing to find a job that met his criteria for a good work–life balance, and he accepted it.

'It's so weird,' he told me a month after starting his new job, 'I used to think that my worth depended on how much I was able to accomplish at work. Looking back at it, though, I see that even though I worked hard, it was never enough. My management didn't value me, and I didn't value myself. When I started setting boundaries at work, my management still didn't value me, but I valued myself enough to recognise that I was mistreated. That allowed me to walk away.'

If ever you feel lonely, burned out, overwhelmed or shamed in your workplace, ask yourself, *Am I being treated kindly by my management? Do I feel like I'm valued? Would I think it's okay for other people to be treated this way?*

And if the answer is 'no', please know that you always have other options.

No job is worth your life, your health or your well-being. You matter and you deserve to be treated like the valuable person you are.

Chapter 31
The Upside Down

In July 2022, I came down with the coronavirus (COVID-19). I expected to have the common symptoms that it stereotypically brings – the fever, shakes, nausea, loss of smell and lethargy.

I was, however, completely unprepared for the devastating whirlwind of depression that showed up as well.

Since the beginning of the pandemic in March 2020, I'd virtually worked with multiple clients before they were exposed, while they were exposed and after they contracted the virus. Because of that, I had personally witnessed people getting struck with the debilitating ramifications of depression and anxiety, as well as unexpected trauma flashbacks, even in clients who were in full remission at the time.

Scientifically speaking, it made sense to me – the virus can lead to a sharp decrease in socialisation and physical activity, which can cause a drop in dopamine, endorphins and oxytocin 'feel good' chemicals in our bodies. In addition, the accompanying nausea, upset stomach and/or appetite changes likely interfere with the body's ability to produce another 'feel good' chemical – serotonin – since 95 per cent of it is made in the gut.[1]

1 Banskota, et al. (2019)

But even though I had seen the psychological effects of COVID impact many clients and had assisted many people with managing these acute spikes in depression and anxiety, I still found myself completely unprepared when it happened to me.

As a trauma survivor and someone who was diagnosed with depression and complex PTSD, the experience of trauma flash-backs isn't new to me. And after years of therapy and working on myself, I believed I could recognise these symptoms and manage them well on my own.

Not this time.

It was as if I had never had therapy. It was as if instead of an independent adult, I was a small defenceless child facing all my inner demons, all at once.

'Are you okay? What's wrong?' my husband Dustin asked when he walked in and found me crying on the couch.

'I'm in the Upside Down,' I managed to say between the sobs.

For those who are unfamiliar, the Upside Down is an alter-nate dimension in the fictional universe of Netflix's *Stranger Things* TV show. When characters get pulled into the Upside Down, their friends and family members cannot reach them, they struggle to be heard, and sometimes cannot be heard at all. A person trapped in the Upside Down might feel frightened and alone, vulnerable to physical and mental attacks by the ter-rible monsters that reside there.

I had my own personal 'Mind Flayer' (a mind-controlling monster in the Upside Down) who told me Dustin would think I was pathetic and a loser. My Mind Flayer also told me that my friends hated me for cancelling my appearance at San Diego

Comic-Con, that my patients would be better off working with a more experienced therapist, that my publisher would walk away from publishing this book, that I'm a terrible person, parent and partner – and mostly, my Mind Flayer told me life is just too damn hard and I don't want to live any more.

All of this was running through my head when I looked at my husband with tears in my eyes, fully expecting his words to match those of my depression monster.

Instead, he held me, and said, 'I've got you. If you're in the Upside Down, then I'm right there with you. And we'll make it out together.'

It was EXACTLY what I needed in that moment. And although my depression and brain fog didn't lift for weeks, being seen, heard and valued by my partner in this way helped me to feel more hopeful at an excruciating moment in my life.

For those of us who struggle with chronic depression, anxiety, suicidal ideation and loneliness, it might feel like we're living in the Upside Down most of the time. And as horrific as those monsters are, they're much more painful when we face them alone or when we are dealing with abusive or invalidating people in our lives. For me, 2022 was a year of heart-wrenching anguish due to the war in my home country, multiple losses of people closest to me, and then the repercussions of COVID.

Through most of it, I was so focused on helping others that I neglected to support myself. Hearing my partner's kind words was a powerful reminder of what I needed. I just needed someone to bear witness to my pain and understand me. Most importantly, I needed someone to sit in the darkness with me, rather than to try to pull me out into the light before I was ready.

So, here are my words to you. If you should find yourself in your own version of the Upside Down, I will sit in the dark with you. Even if we don't know each other, even if we never meet in person, you can imagine me sitting in the dark with you and holding your hand from afar for as long as you need. I've got you and we will get through this together.

Many of us have been taught that when something bad happens to us, we should be 'strong' – pick ourselves up, dust ourselves off and keep going. This implies that if we're going through a break-up, grief or an illness, we're expected to metaphorically slap some duct tape on our emotional, cognitive and physical wounds and carry on.

But does this duct tape effect really mean that we're 'strong'?

Let's think of it in terms of a car. If your car bumper fell off, you could tape it with duct tape and it will hold, at least temporarily.

But what happens when it's your engine that starts having trouble? Or your ignition? Or the brakes? You can imagine what might happen if you tried to repair these problems with duct tape.

Sooner or later your car will need to be repaired properly. You will take it to a mechanic who can fix it – who knows what your car needs to run. And ultimately, if you want your car to take care of you, you must take care of it.

Your body, your heart and your soul have needs, just like

your car does. You cannot expect them to simply keep going without getting the attention they require. If you experience a break-up, a loss, an illness or another traumatic event, your body, heart and soul will need to heal.

Let them.

When you let go of the idea that you must avoid your emotions in order to be 'strong', you will likely feel a great deal of pain, at least at first. This is all the pain that you have been running from coming to the surface because just as you need to be heard and valued, your pain needs to be heard and processed in order for your healing to take place.

This process can be frightening. But know that this pain is just the cracks in your duct tape, which was never meant to hold for this long.

The pain that you feel is your heart breaking free of its bonds.

Let it.

The pain means you are healing. Sometimes we have to break in order to heal. This is what real strength looks like – the courage to face ourselves and our past. The tears that you shed, the anger, the numbness, the depression, the anxiety – this is your body, your heart, and your soul healing.

Let them.

TAKE AWAYS

- Being undervalued refers to being made to feel like you do not matter, like you do not belong, like you are not good enough.

- When we have been undervalued, abused or parentified, we might learn to shame ourselves as a trauma response.

- This might lead you to feel like an outsider or an imposter, and it might mean you use the fawn/people-pleasing response.

- Toxic work environments can wreak havoc on our mental and physical health. If you're feeling ashamed and not good enough at work, it could be because of management.

- You deserve to be valued; it's your right.

- When we first start to heal after years of wearing metaphorical duct tape over our emotional wounds, it will hurt. But this pain will subside and that is when healing really takes place.

- If you feel alone in your own version of the Upside Down, please know that I've got you and we will make it out together.

PART 5:
Forming a Connection with Yourself

Chapter 32
Meeting your Unmet Needs

Over the past four sections we looked at the devastating effects of loneliness on our physical and mental health. We saw how heartbreaking it can be to feel unseen, how invalidating and frustrating it can be to feel unheard, and how much shame, anxiety and resentfulness we carry when we feel undervalued.

These needs – to be seen, heard and valued – are basic human needs. You deserve to have these needs met. And so, in this section, we are going to work on how you can identify your needs and practise meeting them yourself. In the last two sections, we are going to focus on how you can advocate for your needs to others, form a sense of connection and belonging, and align with your sense of purpose.

The reason why it's important to start connection-building with ourselves (as opposed to with other people) is because it allows us to figure out who we are. If we focus on building connections before we get to know ourselves, we can get lost in other people's expectations. On the other hand, when we get to know ourselves and our needs first, we can focus on developing a community that meets our needs.

Another reason to focus on self-connection first is to help you build a sense of *emotional safety*. Having a sense of emotional safety means we feel safe enough to feel and experience our emotions and to express ourselves without the fear of being judged, rejected or humiliated.

How do we build a sense of emotional safety?

A great way to build emotional safety is by learning what our unmet needs are and how to meet them. Most of the stories you've read so far in this book give examples of what having unmet needs might look like. Your unmet needs could include the need to be seen, the need to be heard and validated, the need to be believed, the need for reassurance, the need for safety, the need to feel loved and valued and the need for belonging.

Here are some ways we can practise learning about and meeting our own unmet needs:

1. **Identify a current or a recent situation that made you feel sad, hurt, angry or frustrated.** Sometimes the hardest part of learning to meet your own needs can be knowing what those needs are in the first place. The way you identify an unmet need is by paying attention to how you feel. For example, if you notice that you are feeling irritable, see if you can meet that irritability with gentle curiosity. Ask yourself, *What's making me irritable today? Which of my needs are not being met? What do I need right now?*

2. **Externalise the situation.** Depending on your preference or ability, see if you can either write out what happened or express it verbally or through sign language. Pretend that you're sharing your story either with me or with a trusted confidant.[1]

1 See Neff & Germer (2018) for more information.

3. **Identify your unmet need.** Underneath your feelings of hurt, anger or frustration is a need that someone failed to meet. For example, if you're feeling hurt over being passed up for a promotion at work, your unmet need might be to be seen and to have your efforts recognised. If you are feeling angry that your partner invalidated your needs, your unmet need might be to be heard and validated. If you are feeling stressed out about an upcoming deadline, your unmet need might be rest and support.

4. **Remind yourself that you are not alone in this.** Countless numbers of people have not only been through it too but are also going through it right now. They feel exactly what you feel, and they understand your pain. It makes sense that you feel hurt and frustrated. Anyone in your situation would feel this way. All the people who are in the same situation feel the same way right now, at this very moment. You have every right to feel the way that you do.

5. **Meet your unmet need.** Within you is an inner child who did not have their needs met. Imagine taking this inner child out of your heart or belly and placing them in front of you. If possible, imagine holding their tiny hands in yours or embracing them. See if you can hold them, soothe them, reassure them or tell them something kind and validating to meet their unmet needs; something they long to hear.

Here are some examples:

- I see you
- I hear you
- I believe you
- I believe in you
- I understand you
- I love you
- You were right
- I'm by your side
- I'm in your corner
- I'm with you every step of the way

Regularly engaging in practices like these, where we remind ourselves that we are not alone and can meet our own needs, has been shown to reduce feelings of loneliness.[2] It will take some practice, but over time you can learn to give yourself the validation you need.

This is one of many exercises in this section that were especially designed to help you learn to meet your own needs. Please use whichever exercises work best for you.

I trust you. I trust your wisdom and your intuition to guide you in making the best choices for you.

We're going to get through this together. Try out these exercises for a couple of weeks and note how you're feeling. I'll be with you every step of the way.

2 Borawski & Nowak (2022)

Chapter 33
Getting to Know Yourself

Many of us define ourselves by our achievements or by some of the roles we've had to play. We might think of ourselves as a carer, for example, because we've been made to take care of others while we might have secretly hoped to open an ice-cream parlour in Paris. Or perhaps you identify as being an important manager at a successful company and have been afraid to tell anyone that you secretly hate it and would rather open a small book shop in Barcelona.

Perhaps you've over-identified with painful labels that some sizeist, ableist, racist or otherwise abusive people might have prescribed you, or perhaps you still see yourself as a small defenceless child, and do not see the amazing, courageous person that you are.

Understanding how we define ourselves is important because we tend to feel especially lonely if we have learned to let other people define us and hide who we really are. The truth is that you are already perfect, just the way that you are.

Don't get me wrong, we all make mistakes and we're always growing and changing. And there is nothing you need to do, nothing you need to change about who you really are to be lovable and to belong.

You already are and you already do.

As much as we want to be seen, *really seen*, by another person, many of us have gotten so used to roles we've learned to play that we are terrified of being seen in this way. Because we've been taught that the role that we play is what makes us lovable, we might assume that if someone really got to know us outside of this role, they wouldn't like us.

For example, 'Sarah' was raised in a strict family with rigid gender roles. She was praised for being 'pretty' and for helping her mother with housework. She was chided if she ever brought up the idea of having a job or a career.

Sarah was secretly an artist and was terrified of showing anyone her art. She believed that if she showed it to anyone, they would criticise and discourage her. When her art teacher encouraged her to submit her artwork to a local art competition, Sarah almost didn't do it.

She got first place.

Sarah ended up going to a university and majoring in art, despite her family's objections. She now illustrates comic books, some of them her own.

A few years ago, Sarah met a fan, 'Jasmine', at San Diego Comic-Con. Jasmine told Sarah that she was her favourite artist and that Sarah's work had inspired Jasmine to pursue art as well. Sarah told me later that it was the first time she realised the impact of being seen and recognised for who she truly was as opposed to what her family expected her to become.

Most of us worry so much about what others think of us and trying to fit into the role written for us by another person, that we might be too afraid to step into our own spotlight. This highlights the ultimate dichotomy that many of us face – we both want to be seen and are also terrified of it. Most of us fear that if we were to be really seen for who we are, what we stand for and what we care about, we would be rejected.

And just as we fear being really seen by others, so do most people that we know. Most people worry just as much about what you think of them as you do about what they think of you. This includes our friends, colleagues and even any celebrities you meet. I've seen countless celebrities in treatment who'd agonised for weeks about something they said to a fan, wondering what that fan now thinks of them.

And if all we ever do as human beings is hide who we are and pretend to be someone else, then we're not living our most authentic life. For me in the past, living an inauthentic life meant that I would laugh at jokes I actually found offensive, I would fail to stand up for someone I cared about to appease a bully, I would try to make others happy without considering what made me happy, and I would focus so much on making my parents proud of me that I neglected who I really was. Finding myself allowed me to speak up for what I believe in even when it meant disagreements with others. It meant allowing myself to figure out what truly mattered to me and what kinds of people I wanted to surround myself with. Finding myself allowed me to realise that I have choices.

And you have choices too.

You always have choices. In every situation. They might not always be the choices you find favourable, but you always have choices. And in that regard, you always have control.

By getting to know ourselves, we can learn to recognise the options we have available for what kind of a life we want to lead and how we want to show up for it. By getting to know who we are, we can learn to see, hear and validate ourselves, so that we can notice when these needs aren't met.

Because once you know yourself, then no one can take that away from you. Once you know what you stand for, it doesn't matter if others don't agree. Because once you have the foundation of who you are, you can only grow from there.

This next exercise is for you only. You do not have to share this or show this to anyone else unless you want to.

Please read each question and either write down your answer, practise saying it out loud or say it using sign language. If you don't feel comfortable with any of these methods, please feel free to just silently reflect on possible answers to these questions.

There are no right or wrong answers. This is a process of you getting to know yourself in a safe and compassionate way:

1. Who are you?
2. Who are you *really*? See if you can go a little deeper here.
3. What are the parts of you that most people know?
4. What are the parts of you that only some people know?
5. What are the parts of you that no one knows?
6. If you could share some of the hidden parts of you with a kind and compassionate person, what would you like them to know about you? What would their ideal response be?

7. If you were financially set for ever, what would you do with your life?

8. What did you dream of doing when you were a child?

9. What used to bring you the biggest joy?

10. If you knew with 100 per cent certainty that you'd be good at it, what would you do or try that you haven't yet, or what would you try again?

11. If you didn't fear what people would say or think, what would you do that you aren't doing now?

12. If you could offer some words of kindness and wisdom to a younger version of you, what would you say?

See if you can also think of other questions to get to know yourself better. Get to know yourself the way that you would want to get to know the most interesting person you can think of. Ask yourself the most intimate questions that you've always wanted to ask someone else. You might be surprised at what comes up when you are getting to know yourself in such a way.

Take your time with these. You don't have to answer all of them, and certainly not right away. Spend some time with these questions.

Spend some time with you. The real, magical you. Get to know you. You are worth it.

Chapter 34
The Function of Emotions

The function of your emotions is to let you know what you need. All your emotions play an important role in your well-being. Some of them might be uncomfortable, but they are all necessary. They aren't a sign of weakness; they are the core of your humanity.

Emotions are our feelings, such as sad, angry, happy, excited or anxious. And if we pay attention, we can usually feel them inside our body. For example, anxiety can feel like nausea, like pressure in the chest or a dropping feeling in the stomach. Some emotions feel similar to others – for example, anxiety and excitement feel similar to one another physically, in terms of our pounding heart and shortness of breath.[1] The same can be said for repressed rage being mistaken for panic attacks.

Here are some examples of emotions we might experience, as well as their function (what role they play in helping us survive) and examples of situations in which we might feel this way. See if you can recognise any of these emotions and think about situations in which you've felt them.

1 Brown (2021)

The Function of Emotions

Emotion	Function	Example
Anger	To protect ourselves or others and take a protective or caring action	When you or someone else is being mistreated
Depression	To let us know that we need to stop, rest and heal, reminding us to seek support or to support ourselves	When you are lonely, rejected or heartbroken
Disgust	To avoid toxic foods or people	When you learn about someone's immoral actions
Empathy	To feel with someone else, to help and better understand others, to foster connection	When you feel sad learning about someone else's grief, or feel joy about their success
Frustration	To preserve or expel energy when things are not going the way you would like or need	When someone repeatedly ignores you
Guilt	To learn which actions might not be helpful in the future	When you feel bad about saying something unkind in an argument
Happiness/Joy	To give our lives meaning, to remind us of what we care about the most	When someone truly notices you and your efforts, when you engage in an activity that brings you pleasure
Hate	Comes from pain, functions to try to protect us from further pain	When someone severely hurts you or someone you care about

Hopefulness	To motivate and inspire change, to give us something to look forward to	When you start a new treatment strategy for an illness, when you start a new career or a new relationship
Hopelessness	To alert us that something is not working, and we need to try something new	When you realise that avoidance does not take away your emotional or physical pain
Irritability	To signal to us that we might be burning out or not getting enough support	When you snap at someone even though they didn't do anything wrong
Jealousy	To look for reassurance and to seek emotional safety	When you compare yourself to others or fear losing someone
Overwhelm	To signal to us that we need support or guidance	When you have too many things to do and don't have enough resources (time, energy or money) to complete them all
Panic/Anxiety	To alert us that we need to rest, cry, vent or seek emotional safety or reassurance, as well as a reminder to slow down and process what we are going through	When you have too many things to do and not enough time to do them; when you think that you are not good enough, or when you have not processed past grief or trauma
Rage	To express ourselves, to be heard, and to use our voice	When someone repeatedly disregards you and makes you feel insignificant and unimportant

Resentment	To inform us that our needs aren't being met	When a co-worker takes a vacation, and you haven't had time off in years
Shame	To avoid being rejected, to belong, to establish connection with others	When you do something that goes against your core values or the values of your collective
Surprise	To alert us to new information, to keep us out of danger	When you see someone or something you didn't expect
Vulnerability	To connect with others, to build emotional closeness and safety	When you open up to yourself and others about how you feel

Take some time this week getting to know your emotions.

Name them. Don't judge them. Instead, see if you can study them with curiousity.

Feel them.

See if they are trying to tell you something.

See if you can reflect with kindness about what your emotions are trying to say. Are they perhaps indicating that you have certain unmet needs? If so, what are they?

Your needs are valid, and they deserve to be met. So, let's figure out what they are.

Chapter 35
Grounding

Sometimes our emotions feel overwhelming. This is especially true if we've spent most of our lives repressing them. In addition, because emotions live *in the body*, we sometimes associate certain physiological sensations with trauma or danger even when we're not literally in danger in the moment.[1]

For example, at one point I was a victim of a violent crime. While it was happening, my heart pounded in my chest. My body froze. I felt like I couldn't breathe and my vision blurred. For years after it happened, I felt a sense of panic when experiencing the same sensations, even if my heart was pounding because I was dancing or going for a run.

Years later, I learned about grounding exercises, and they have been life-changing for me. Grounding is a self-soothing technique that we can utilise when we feel triggered or overwhelmed. It is a way of keeping your focus in the present moment rather than in a flashback from your past or an imagined future scenario.

Here are some grounding practices:

1.   If possible, notice the sensation of your feet. Ask

1 van der Kolk (2014)

yourself, *Where are my feet?* Feel your feet making contact with the ground. Remind yourself that in this very moment, you are safe. If the sensation of your feet is not available to you, you can instead use the sensation of your hands, the sensation of your seat or the sensation of your lips for grounding.

2. Focus on one of your senses, such as your sense of touch. You can hold a piece of ice, a rock, a piece of jewellery or something else that can help you to keep focus on feeling that object.

3. Focus on the uncomfortable sensation such as your racing heart, set your timer for three minutes and gently breathe. With each exhale, imagine soothing this sensation. Repeat as necessary. Then switch to another uncomfortable sensation in your body.

4. Focus on something that is happening right now. For example, notice the colours of the cars passing by or notice the sounds that you hear right now.

5. Practise grounding to the present moment. Ask yourself, *What's today's date?*, *What time is it?*, *Where am I right now?* and *Am I safe in this very moment?*

These practices can help you to recognise that today, in this very moment, you are safe, even though you weren't safe in the past.[2]

---

2 If you are currently physically unsafe, please get yourself to safety whenever possible

These exercises are intended to help you feel grounded in the present moment, which can bring relief from overwhelming emotions. It can be helpful to first practise them when you feel less overwhelmed, so that when you need to utilise them, you've already had some experience.

In fact, practising noticing your physiological sensations when you are not overwhelmed can make it easier for you to practise them at other times. Many trauma survivors do not feel safe or comfortable experiencing certain sensations in their body. For instance, survivors of sexual assault sometimes disconnect from feeling any sensations in their genital area. In addition, many trauma survivors feel overwhelmed and uncomfortable when they notice their internal sensations, such as the sensation of their breathing, stomach discomfort or the feeling of their racing heart.[3]

None of these sensations are actually dangerous; in fact, these are the same sensations we feel when we are excited, such as when we are dancing, exercising, cheering for our favourite sports team or otherwise enjoying ourselves. However, we might feel unsafe in our body when we have these experiences because these same sensations might have been present when something terrible was happening to us.

And so the same pounding heart that was happening when we were bullied or abused might make us feel unsafe when we are exercising or enjoying ourselves at a comedy show. And if our body feels unsafe when our heart starts to beat faster

3 Levine (2010)

even if we are now in a safe situation, then we will experience a sense of a false alarm, even if logically we know that nothing is wrong.

Please know that this experience is common and completely normal. It takes time for your body to learn to feel safe in these situations again.

If purposely noticing your internal sensations in this way feels unsafe or uncomfortable in the moment, please take a break and try again later. Just like a newly adopted kitten or a puppy who has been abused and injured, your nervous system needs to learn to trust you over time in order to feel safe.

Your nervous system will need to learn that experiencing your internal body sensations is safe, and good for you. Learning to feel the changes in the muscle tension in your jaw, shoulders, arms or legs can help you to breathe and purposely release some of this built-up tension. Learning to experience the changes in your breathing, the changes in your heart rate, and your stomach sensations can help you to learn to better navigate these experiences and to know what your body needs.

Take your time. Go slow.

I know that sometimes you might want to just distract yourself and not feel anything. And that's okay. It makes sense. Feeling your internal sensations can be hard work, and we all need a break sometimes. Also, perhaps it hasn't always been safe for you to feel your emotions and physical sensations. Perhaps your past coping behaviours, healthy or not, saved your life. I'm glad that they did, and I'm glad that you're here.

If you decide to try grounding exercises, just do what you

can. No need to push yourself beyond your limits. And if you're not ready, that's okay too.

Go as slowly as you need to. Over time, feeling your body and grounding can actually help you to feel safer and more present, even if today these sensations may feel uncomfortable. Take your time. There is no rush. This is your process.

I trust you.

I honour you.

And I'm here in your corner.

Chapter 36
Timeline of Your Life

I'm often surprised at how frequently my clients – the bravest, most courageous people I've ever met – struggle to see their own accomplishments. This is true of many trauma survivors.

As if wearing muddy glasses, trauma creates a skewed view of ourselves, only allowing us to see glimpses of who we are and what we've overcome. This is where a timeline exercise comes in.

A timeline is a combination of the most significant events our life – in particular, the struggles we overcame, as well as the wonderful experiences we went through. Like separate puzzle pieces scattered all over the floor, different elements of our life can leave us feeling fragmented, as opposed to allowing us to see the full, integrated picture of our life experience.

Most of us might be fascinated with our heroes, real or fictional, largely because we've gotten to know them from the place of curiosity, as if they are the most interesting person in the world. And what if you got to know yourself the same way, as if you were the most interesting person in the world? Because you are – the most interesting person in the world. By getting to know yourself, *really* getting to know yourself, you might be able to see things from a different perspective. You might be able to remember times that you did not think you would get through but did. You might be able to see how you've not only survived, you've *thrived* and will thrive for years to come.

Let's try it out. There are many ways to complete the timeline exercise. One way to do it is to write down (or verbally list) the most significant events of your life. Only you get to decide what constitutes a 'significant' event for you.

You can write it out in brief bullet points. For example:

- Age 5 – got a puppy
- Age 5 – grandpa died
- Age 8 – big fight with Mom
- Age 8 – got bullied
- Age 8 – stood up for myself
- Age 9 – fun birthday party

See if you can write out or draw your own timeline. Start at your earliest memory and keep going all the way until now. Write out all the significant events you can remember, especially the extremes – the really painful ones and the really special ones – as well as ones where you persevered or stood up for something or someone. Write as many as you can remember while providing just a few words for each one; no need to go into details. Feel free to write it all at once or in small chunks over several days or weeks.

Once you've completed your timeline, consider the following questions:

- What are some patterns that you noticed?

- How do you feel in your body when you think about these events? Can you breathe into the part of the body that feels tense, stiff or achy at the moment? You might be holding your trauma there. Roll your shoulders back, breathe to release some of the tension from your jaw, chest and stomach. If possible, stretch out and loosen up your arms and legs. Being aware of our body in this way, and releasing some of the stored tension we are carrying, can help us to also release some of the trauma we hold there.

- Can you consider some of the events you remembered from an empowered perspective? What did you overcome? How did you stand up for yourself – perhaps by walking away from a difficult situation, by getting help or otherwise changing things to support yourself?

- Can you imagine protecting yourself back then? Can you pantomime protecting yourself? Act it out – pretend to push someone away, pretend to run away, take yourself out of that situation, or imagine that you can travel back in time and speak up for yourself. What would you say to protect and validate yourself?

- Who were your friends and support systems?

- What have been some empowered or resilient steps that you have taken to care for yourself since then? For example, cancelling plans because you are tired, reaching out to friends, attending support groups or reading self-help books are all steps to empower yourself.

- How have you helped others over time?

Take some time to reflect on your timeline by answering some of these questions. See if you can practise meeting your unmet needs and grounding exercises as you do so. For example, if you remembered a painful fight with a close friend, see if you still feel hurt about it. See if you can offer yourself some kind words or a hug. See if you can verbally express everything you wanted to say at that time but didn't get a chance to. Allow yourself to fully express yourself. Hear yourself out. Validate yourself, for example, *I'm so sorry. That really hurt. You deserved better. I'm with you, we are going to get through this together.*

Take your time with this.

Remember that you are healing.

You are not alone in this. I'm here with you. We will get through this together.

Chapter 37

HSP Unicorns

I knew I was a highly sensitive person (HSP) before I had ever heard the term.

When I was a child, I used to think that something was wrong with me. Other kids seemed to make friends easily, while I didn't. Other kids seemed to enjoy loud music and crowded get-togethers, while I would get severely overstimulated by them and want to leave. Loud noises and bright lights would not only trigger my migraines, but they also made me want to run away and hide, so I did. And there, in a quiet, dimly lit room of my house, wrapped in a thick heavy blanket, hugging my pillow or my teddy bear, I would find peace.

Many of us HSPs get overstimulated by bright lights, loud noises and violent scenes on TV. HSPs are likely to be criticised and called 'too sensitive'. Many of us also worry about offending other people and often agonise over social interactions.

HSP is not a medical or a mental health disorder, but some HSPs might additionally be diagnosed with PTSD, sensory processing disorder, autism, ADHD, autoimmune disorders or migraines. For more information about HSPs, check out Dr Elaine Aron's book *The Highly Sensitive Person*.[1]

1 Aron (2013)

Some HSPs are also empaths – people who have the ability to feel the emotions of other living beings. Being both an HSP and an empath is rare, with HSPs constituting approximately 20 per cent of the global population and empaths only 1–2 per cent.[2] As a result, many HSPs and empaths feel very lonely.

Many empaths have a sense of connection with plants or animals.[3] Many empaths also feel the energy around them, such as feeling sad when the weather changes, or experiencing heart palpitations on a busy highway or at loud concerts. This happens because empaths literally resonate with the stimuli around them and match their energy. This is why many empaths are so drained when attending busy and fast-paced events, such as large parties, concerts or when travelling in a busy airport.

As an HSP and an empath, I get really overwhelmed when in a loud, populated environment, such as a busy restaurant or an airport. I get very overstimulated with bright lights, loud sounds and feeling everyone's emotions around me.

It's for this reason that I created the 'Bubble Up' exercise, although similar versions of it exist in many self-help books.

To practise the 'Bubble Up' exercise, start by taking a few slow breaths.

Find your centre by feeling the sensation of your feet, or the sensation of your lower back, hips or pelvis rooting you in your seat, or the pressure of your lips. Return to one of these sensations any time you feel like you need to practise grounding again, to return to attending to your own needs in this moment.

2 Aron (2013); Orloff (2017)
3 Orloff (2017)

Then, imagine building a wide, thick, clear energy bubble around yourself. This bubble moves with you as you move.

Your energy stays on the inside of the bubble. Other people's energy stays on the outside of your bubble.

Breathe.

Keep imagining the bubble. What colour is it? Some people like to imagine that the bubble is clear, while others like to imagine a golden or a silver bubble, or a purple one. What colour would your protective bubble have?

What would be its texture?

How thick would it be?

When noise, energy or bright lights bump up against your bubble, how does it respond? How does your bubble keep you safe?

Keep breathing, keep visualising this bubble.

This bubble can help to protect your energy, can reduce your levels of overwhelm and overstimulation, and can allow you to feel safer and more grounded inside of it.

Reset your bubble hourly or as often as you need to. You deserve to feel safe and to protect your energy.

If you're an HSP, an empath, or both, chances are that you'd been misunderstood and criticised for being 'too sensitive' or not being able to 'just let things go'. And it is for this reason that many of us feel lonely. Chances are that, like me, you probably spent most of your life feeling like you're different.

And that's because you are.

Whether you're an empath, an HSP or you fall into a differ-ent category, you are both the same and different. You are the same as everyone else in a sense that most people feel like they are an outsider at some point in their life, even if they don't speak of it.

And you are also different because of your abilities – whether it is your ability to empathise with others or to resonate with your environment, you *are* different. This is your superpower. I think it's what makes you especially unique and wonderful.

And maybe your entire life, people have been trying to define you and put you into a metaphorical box of their own making by telling you how you should think, feel and act.

But maybe you are a unicorn. And everyone knows that unicorns do not belong in boxes.

So, please, in a world full of boxes, be a unicorn. Do not suppress your superpower. Instead, let your magic be your guide.

Chapter 38
Self–soothing

If you've ever had a broken arm, then you probably remember that a doctor had to carefully put it into a protective cast while it healed.

And when it's your heart that's broken, we need to carefully wrap it in a hug and give it time to heal too.

So, if you're hurting today, if you are going through a loss or processing something painful from long ago, know that your heart and your body both deserve to be treated with love, care and kindness while you heal. If there is a loving person or a pet around you, see if you can hug them as a way to care for your-self. And if there is not another person or a pet around, you can learn to self-soothe and meet this critical emotional need yourself. Your body has a natural self-soothe response, and you can learn how to activate it.

Let's try it out.

If you are willing, please grab a blanket, ideally a thick com-forter or a weighted blanket, but any blanket will do. And also, please grab either a pillow or a stuffed animal. Your choice.

Once you've got your blanket and your pillow or stuffed animal, sit in as comfortable a posture as you can. If sitting is either painful or not physically possible, then please lie down, or get into any posture that supports your body.

Please wrap the blanket around you. If possible, please have it cover your shoulders and your back, where the back of your heart is, but if you'd rather reposition your blanket in any way or not use it at all, that's okay too.

Get as comfortable as possible.

Now, please hug the pillow or the stuffed animal to your chest and stomach. If possible, see if you can turn the pillow the long way, so that it hugs both your chest and stomach at the same time. See if you can gently squeeze the pillow or the stuffed animal as a kind self-hug.[1]

Putting mild pressure, like a hug, on your chest and stomach activates the release of oxytocin (our natural self-soothing hormone) and your body's overall soothing response.

See if you can stay in this gentle hug posture for about three minutes, but feel free to shift or change your posture in any way you need to support your body.

You deserve kindness.

You deserve gentleness.

You deserve comfort and support.

---

1 See Neff (2011) and Neff (2021) for more self-soothing practices and exercises.

Chapter 39
Appointments with Grief

Grief arises in many forms, and we grieve in many situations.

We grieve after someone dies. But we also grieve after a loss of a relationship, even if the other person was toxic or abusive. It is possible to intentionally cut someone out of our lives and miss them as well. As human beings, we are complex, and therefore can experience seemingly opposite emotions at the same time, such as grief and relief. All of these emotions make sense, including grief. This is why when someone tries to cheer us up by telling us that we should be feeling 'happy that it's over', we feel unseen because the other person fails to acknowledge grief as an important part of our experience.

We might grieve the loss of a job or an opportunity we didn't get a chance to have. We might grieve not having had a 'normal' childhood, especially if we were abandoned, abused or parentified.

We might grieve the loss of an ability, such as the ability to walk, see or hear. We might grieve the loss of ourselves when we've abandoned who we are to try to fit into someone else's narrative. And we might grieve the loss of an object that holds a sentimental value to us.

We stereotypically think of grief as an emotion of sadness. But grief is vast and diverse in its presentation.

Grief can also show up as anger, rage, envy, irritability, panic attacks, guilt, shame, regret or apathy.

However your grief shows up is okay. This is your heart trying to make sense of the painful experiences you endured. It doesn't matter how long it's been since the event occurred. There is no timeline on grief, which means that you can take as much time with it as you need to.

People who say that we heal from grief over time are wrong. We don't heal FROM grief.

We heal WITH it.

We heal AROUND it.

We heal INSIDE it.

We keep it in our heart forever and it helps us to grow, to become a wiser and a more compassionate person.

We also heal grief by honouring it. The best way we can honour grief is by intentionally spending time with it.

My favourite way of spending time with grief is a practice I call Appointments with Grief.

Here are the steps to practise:

1. Don't wait for your grief to overwhelm you. This grief isn't coming. It's already here. And you can either wait for its tidal wave to overwhelm you at the most inconvenient time or you can make intentional appointments with it on your schedule.

2. Choose a time of day to practise having your

appointments with grief. For the first month of going through a loss, I recommend daily practices, and after that, as often as needed.

3. When you are ready to start practising, go to a quiet place where you can be alone and undisturbed for three to five minutes.

4. Set your timer for three minutes and press *start*.

5. During these three minutes, let it all out. Whatever you are feeling – sadness, anger, irritability – all of it. Cry if you need to. Scream or wail if you need to. Howl if you can. Whisper cry if you can't be loud at the moment.

     Write. Vent. Sing.

     Let it all out.

     Unleash it all.

     And if nothing happens, that's okay too. If you feel no emotions, that's all right. You might be too tapped out right now and might be feeling numb as a result. Whatever you feel or don't feel, just notice that. Observe it for three minutes and allow your mind and body to notice the chaos or the stillness that comes up without any judgement.

6. Once the three minutes are up, feel free to stop, but if you need more time, keep going.

7. Take time to self-soothe right after – give yourself a hug, watch an old episode of a favourite show, listen to a song you like; anything you can do to really support yourself. The goal of this step isn't to take away your pain. The goal of this step is to practise soothing and supporting yourself WHILE you're in pain.

8. Repeat daily for one month and then as needed. With future losses, repeat daily for a month again, and then again, as needed.

If you ever find this exercise too overwhelming or too triggering, you do not have to force yourself to get through it. White-knuckling through emotional experiences is neither necessary nor helpful. Self-compassion researchers Kristin Neff and Chris Germer suggest that sometimes when we are too exhausted, too overwhelmed, or are in too much pain to be open to our emotions, we might need to close our emotional door, meaning that we need to step back for a bit until we're well enough to continue.[1]

So, if you find that, at any point of this exercise, you are feeling too triggered or too overwhelmed, then please give yourself the permission to close by stopping this practice, stepping away or focusing on something else. You can always come back to this exercise later.

You deserve to be seen, heard and valued by others. And also, by your own self. You deserve this kind of fierce love and compassion for yourself where you can bear witness to your own pain and practise supporting yourself.[2]

You deserve to unleash your grief and pain instead of being imprisoned by it. I see your pain. I know it's hard. I so wish I could take it away from you. I know that I can't, but I will hold your hand in the process. We will get through this together.

1 Neff & Germer (2018)
2 Neff (2021)

Chapter 40
Spoons and Batteries

When your phone, computer or tablet run low on battery, you probably plug them in to recharge.

And similarly, when we are depleted, we need to recharge.

Since we humans don't have a battery bar to tell us when we need recharging, you'll need to check in with yourself as frequently as you are able, daily if you can, or even once an hour. Ask yourself, *Out of 100 per cent, what's my internal battery charge right now?*

Some people prefer using the concept of *spoons* from the Spoon Theory.[1] The spoons here are a metaphor for our mental health and physical health in terms of available inner resources. If someone says that they have twelve spoons, this indicates that they are fully charged up (at 100 per cent) and feel rested. If someone is out of spoons (at 0 per cent), this means they are fully depleted and can't function.

If at all possible, we want to try to keep our batteries above 50 per cent at all times (or above six spoons). We do not have to wait to get to zero to recharge. Think of it as *energy economics*. If you only have a small amount of energy to spend, then you might need to be careful of how you spend it. It would be unwise

1 Miserandino (2003)

217

to overspend your energy by forcing yourself to do more than you are able because then you will likely find yourself in energy debt and will need to take more time to recover later.

Many of us who are going through grief, trauma, loneliness, depression or chronic illness start our day with fewer spoons than other people. We might also deplete quicker than others. Unfortunately, some of us are also more likely to experience ableist oppression that we discussed in Chapter 20, where some people might tell us that we just 'need to be stronger' or accuse us of being 'lazy' or faking our symptoms. If this happens to you, please don't let other people gaslight you out of your reality. Your symptoms are real, and you deserve to rest and recharge when you need to.

It's okay if you have frequently let your inner battery fully drain before charging up again. I used to do it too. I used to think that I must finish all my work before I was allowed to rest.

As a result, I was always depleted or on the verge of depletion.

It took me a long time to accept the fact that recharging is not being lazy. It is a necessary investment into building up and replenishing my inner resources, so that I can have the energy that I need to function.

This process is not easy, and it does not happen overnight. But know that you are working on it, and you are healing.

There's no one set way to recharge. The main point of recharging is to replenish your spoons or your inner battery. Ask yourself, *What do I need right now to recharge?*

Here are some ideas:

- Eat something
- Hydrate
- Take a nap
- Go for a walk
- Take some non-verbal time to unwind (more on this in the next chapter)
- Catch up with a friend
- Watch a few episodes of your favourite show
- Play some video or phone games
- Watch cute kitten or puppy videos
- Read a book for fun

When I teach about these recharge activities in my workshops, someone will inevitably ask me if such recharge practices will lead to procrastination and laziness. And here the research says *no*. The more we practise self-kindness and self-compassion, the less stressed we become, the less we procrastinate,[2] and the more energy we then have to complete our tasks.

The same activity, such as reading a fun book, watching our favourite show or playing video games, can have a different effect depending on why we're engaging in it. When we watch TV or play games to procrastinate doing our work, we are likely to watch or play longer, feeling guilty and demotivated after. But when we do it on purpose, when we tell ourselves, 'I'm going to watch two episodes of this show to rest and recharge and then I will get to my work,' we are more likely to honour this plan and to feel more motivated afterward.

2 Neff (2011) and Sirois (2014)

The activities we talked about so far can be helpful for recharging in the short term. A helpful way of recharging our internal batteries in the long term is to analyse our *pie chart*. Much like we can measure our reserve of energy using spoons or batteries, we can also think of the way that we allocate and use our energy as a pie chart.

For example, if we're allocating 100 per cent of our energy towards one person, then our well-being is completely dependent on how things are going with that individual. So, when the relationship is going well, we feel happy. However, when there is a conflict, it's as if 100 per cent of our world has collapsed.

One way to create a healthier, more robust balance in our lives is to balance out the pie chart of your life. This way, even if one of the pieces of your pie chart isn't going well, you have others to fall back on.

Here's an example of what your pie chart might look like:

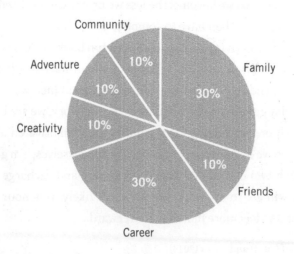

To create your own energy pie chart, first list the aspects of your life that are important to you. It doesn't matter if you still devote your attention to these aspects or if you've neglected them for a while. Just make a list.

Examples of important aspects might include your relationships, health, creativity, career, community, helping others and fun.

Once you have made a list of all the aspects of your life that you value, try labelling each area with a percentage that represents how much of your time and energy you devote to each area right now. Then, fill in the pie chart on a separate sheet of paper, with the corresponding percentages of your waking time. Try to make it add up to a 100 per cent.

For example, if you currently spend 80 per cent of your waking time working and 15 per cent with your family and 5 per cent with your friends, you might not have time for much else. Sometimes, we are hard on ourselves for not being able to fit in all of our desired activities but may fail to realise that, with our current schedules, all our available time is already taken.

Take a few moments to fill out your pie chart as it represents your allocation of your time this week.

Now, notice which areas of your life are missing or aren't getting as much attention as you would like. See if you can redraw the pie chart now to represent how you would ideally like it to look, even if you aren't yet sure how to make it all work. For example, perhaps you'd ideally like to decrease the amount of time and energy you're allocating to work from

80 per cent to 60 per cent, to increase the amount of time you're spending with your friends from 5 per cent to 10 per cent, and to fit in a creative activity (at let's say 5 per cent), add intentional rest time (10 per cent), and still spend 15 per cent of your time with your family. So, draw that adjusted pie chart on a separate piece of paper.

If you're unable to draw or shade in the pie chart, simply reflect on how you might want to divide up your time to make room for activities that you find meaningful.

In order for this new idealised pie chart to come to fruition in the future (say, one year from now or even ten years from now), what small steps would you need to take today to make that happen? Perhaps if you normally work late, you might step away fifteen minutes earlier on one of the days this week and call a dear friend instead? Perhaps you can look into a trip you'd like to take next year or consider different volunteering opportunities, even if you're not yet ready to commit to them.

This week, see if you can take some small steps towards balancing out your pie chart.

You deserve a fulfilling and a balanced life. You are worth it.

Chapter 41
Compassionate Solitude

'How much time out of your day do you spend in a quiet solitude?' Erin, my wonderful book coach, once asked me.

She was trying to help me return to my writing after I was struggling with a stretch of a creative block.

I was stunned. 'Well, none.'

It wasn't just that the obvious answer was 'none' that shocked me. It was that I hadn't ever even considered the question before she asked me.

My schedule at that time involved rolling out of bed at 6 a.m., rushing to get ready for work, seeing ten to twelve clients per day, spending one to two hours doing additional work, and then rushing to spend the last hour of the day with my family. On weekends, I would see some clients on an emergency basis, teach, write, or catch up with friends and colleagues. There was no unscheduled time, and, more importantly, no time when I wasn't speaking, listening, reading or writing.

I had never considered that for an empath and a highly sensitive person, a schedule like this would cause overstimulation and burnout. As a creative, my writing suffered because I didn't have any time to recharge my creative energy.

Tears burned my eyes as I realised how much I had neglected

myself. 'But my schedule is so packed that there's just no time for me, for at least the next six months.'

Erin gave me an empathetic smile. 'I get it. And I definitely don't want to add to the pressure you already have. So, how about this – give me twenty minutes per day of non-verbal time. If twenty doesn't work, give me fifteen. If that doesn't work then give me ten, or whatever you can do.'

Non-verbal time is time intentionally taken for solitude and rest. It can include drawing, painting, stretching, a quiet meditation, a walk by yourself, taking a shower, etc. The only requirements are that this activity is done in solitude (pets are okay) and without any words (so, no reading, no talking, no writing, and no listening to anything with words or lyrics. If you are a visual artist, it also means no drawing or painting, since the idea is to take a break from your usual activities).

Because our brain works hard to process information all day long, the best way we can let our brain rest is to remove some stimulation from it. Non-verbal time allows your brain to rest and recharges your creative battery.

Sometimes, as we start spending more time in solitude, we remember past traumas or realise that some of our current conditions aren't working.

It can be helpful to keep a journal for 'brain dumping' before or after your non-verbal time. Some people benefit from writing before starting their non-verbal time, so that they can relax after. Others like to observe and subsequently reflect about what came up for them during their non-verbal time. This type of reflection journaling can be written, typed, drawn or spoken out loud. There's no wrong way of doing it. The point of it is to help you reflect and continue to get to know yourself.

Another way to practise managing some of the thoughts, feelings and physical sensations that might come up for you during your non-verbal time is the Dog in the Park exercise from Chapter 22 or practising the three-minute Appointments with Grief exercise from Chapter 39.

In my case, when I started practising non-verbal time (usually by either doodling or listening to meditative music without lyrics), I found that I was thinking more clearly afterward, I was more patient with my family and my creativity returned and blossomed. We all need a mental recharge. Yours does not have to look the same as mine. You might go for a walk or look at pretty pictures or play with your pet or find another exercise to practise.

Try it out. Give your brain a rest, especially from the kind of strain you're usually under. Try it for twenty minutes per day for several weeks, if you can. If twenty is impossible, do what you can.

This is YOUR time to spend healing and resting in the way that works for you. Take it. You deserve it and you are worth it.

Chapter 42
Savouring and Self-appreciation

One of the best ways we can manage loneliness is through mindfulness. To be *mindful* means *noticing* – noticing our external environment and our internal experiences without judging them as 'good or bad' but rather just observing them as they are. We can use mindfulness to notice when we have an unmet need or when we feel depleted, so as to better support ourselves.

We can also use mindfulness to enjoy some of our experiences. This is called *savouring*. An example of savouring is enjoying a cup of ice cream and noticing how delicious it tastes. We might even close our eyes to focus on really tasting it.

Other examples of savouring include noticing the soothing taste of the first sip of your morning tea or coffee, listening to your favourite song, watching a beautiful sunrise without interruptions, pausing to notice the sound of your loved one's laugh, seeing your pet run around with joy, or the way it feels to snuggle under cosy blankets.

Savouring is essentially a practice of mindfully appreciating the present moment. This practice can allow us to foster a sense of connection with our environment and with ourselves.

Another type of mindfulness practice is *self-appreciation*. Some of us generously dole out appreciative comments to others but only offer harsh criticisms to ourselves. It's no wonder we feel lonely under these circumstances – we feel unseen and undervalued by our own self.

In first hearing about self-appreciation, some people understandably worry that this practice will make them selfish or conceited. However, just like recharging our inner batteries or learning how to meet our own unmet needs, the practice of self-appreciation makes us kinder and more compassionate. Once we're able to meet our own needs for support, rest and deep appreciation, we have more internal resources available to offer this support to others.[1]

One way we can practise self-appreciation is to compliment and celebrate ourselves. For example, I might say to myself, 'Great job, rockstar!' when I've written another chapter of my book.

Another way you can practise self-appreciation is by leaving a sticky note for yourself with a kind and a supportive message. For example, I have written things like, 'I promise I'll make time for you today,' and, 'You make a difference, don't ever forget that.'

My book coach, Erin, shared with me that she leaves loving sticky notes for her future self from her past self. For example, she might leave a note for herself that says, 'Erin, your lunch is packed and ready in the fringe. Love, Past Erin.' She says that the next day she finds herself feeling grateful to read these notes and also practises gratitude by saying something along the lines of, 'Wow, thanks, past Erin!' Creating such a kind

1 Neff & Pommier (2013)

and compassionate dialogue with yourself can allow you to befriend yourself, potentially reducing feelings of loneliness and increasing the feelings of belonging.

Finally, you can make or buy yourself something nice, either *just because* or to celebrate something. You can get yourself a new plant or some flowers, a nice candle, a new book, or a game, or perhaps you can look up pretty pictures of sunrises or sunsets on the internet, look at kitten or puppy videos, or doodle. The *What* you get doesn't matter so much as the *Why* you get it – to celebrate you, to honour you, and to appreciate you. You can take yourself on a nice walk and pick up a pretty rock along the way, or reserve yourself a nice massage, or take yourself out to your favourite restaurant.

Date yourself!

Think of what you might do for someone you really love, someone really special, and *do that for yourself.* Remember to allow yourself to take the time to savour it.

You don't have to do anything to earn it. You already have.

Chapter 43
Guidance from Your Hero

As a way of building a relationship with yourself, you can tap into your inner wisdom.

Deep inside, you know what you need to do and what you very much need to hear. Undoubtedly, letting yourself truly see and hear yourself can make you feel raw and very vulnerable. The more raw and vulnerable you feel about what you discover, the more you know that it is the very information you need to get to the core of your inner truth.

One way you can practise tapping into your inner wisdom is through the 'Guidance from Your Hero' exercise.

Guidance from Your Hero

Take a few moments to think about a personal hero. This is someone you see as a figure of ultimate wisdom, kindness and compassion. This could be a real person – such as a grandparent (even if they are no longer alive), a teacher, a mentor, an athlete, a creative – or a historical figure you look up to. Or it could be a fictional character.

If you cannot think of a personal hero, consider what kind of qualities your hero would have. Imagine a human being, an animal, a spiritual figure or an energy presence that is warm, caring and kind.

Imagine that you have some alone time with your compassionate hero. Your hero knows exactly what you have been through. Your hero is kind, supportive and encouraging. Your hero knows exactly the best thing to say to you and what you really need to hear.

What would your hero say to you?

Perhaps your hero might remind you that you've been through many challenges, and so it makes sense that you are feeling the way you are feeling right now. Perhaps your hero would remind you that there have been many times when you thought you wouldn't be able to survive something or get through it, and then you did. Perhaps your hero would let you know that you have a purpose here. That your being here helps other people. They might remind you that you matter, that they love you and care about you, and that they are with you every step of the way.

Try this out whenever you are facing a challenging situation, even a seemingly 'trivial' one. This practice is about building and channelling your inner wisdom and self-compassion.

Remember that this exercise can take time and practice. If you try it and you are not able to think of what your hero would say to you, no problem. It happens to a lot of people. It might mean that you need to close your emotions for today as an act of self-compassion. And that's okay.

Take a breath. Concentrate on imagining that your hero is with you, that they love you, that they're in your corner, and try the exercise another time. In the meantime, consider writing in your journal about how you are feeling, practising the

Dog in the Park exercise or taking a three-minute appointment with your grief.

Remember that we don't only feel grief when someone dies. We also feel grief when relationships end, when friendships fall apart, when we realise that we didn't have the kind of childhood that we deserved or the kind of support we needed.

That's grief, too.

And your hero knows that and sees that. They care for you and are here to support you whenever you are ready for them by giving you the compassion, reassurance and encouragement that you need. They know exactly what you need to hear and the kind of support you need at this time, including a reminder that you have dealt with challenges before, you are more powerful than you realise and you will get through this.

With practice, you will be able to tap into this inner wisdom whenever you need it. You deserve it and you are worth it.

Chapter 44
'I'll Be Happy When . . .'

For much of my life, I always thought that I have to do every-thing quickly and *now* – that I have to graduate *now*, that I have to publish all my books *now*, that I have to change the way I look *now*.

I've always told myself that I'll be happy *when* . . . I told myself that I'll be happy *when* I graduate. That I'll be happy *when* I move to California. *When* I get licensed. *When* I publish my book. *When* I pay off my student loans. *When* I lose weight.

Like a sadistic game of carrot on the stick, I'd single-hand-edly made my own happiness unattainable, something I had to wait to receive, only to then create another moving target.

It can be easy to spend a majority of our lives waiting to live. And in the meantime, we run an exhausting race to get there as soon as possible.

In 2022, after the war in my home country broke out, I was so devastated that I had no choice but to focus on my grief. I tried to ignore it and put on my 'I am fine' metaphorical mask but the grief won out. The more I tried to mask up, the more anxious and irritable I felt. That is until I allowed myself to sob. After that, I started making daily three-minute appointments with my grief, focusing on slowing down, and taking extra time to engage in my non-verbal practices. As a result, I was able to slow down enough to realise that I desperately needed to rest and recharge.

Giving myself the permission not only to recharge but to cut back on my work was a personal and a very important choice, and it happened while I was attempting to write this very book. It was due to my editor on the first of October. My ego and my pride have prevented me from asking for extensions when I needed them. However, this time, I knew I needed to ask for more time. In July 2022 – during the war in Ukraine, while having COVID, and still seeing patients virtually, as well as teaching and writing – I knew that something had to give.

My choices were to speed up and push myself to finish this book while writing it on autopilot, or to ask for an extension, slow down and write it from the heart. And so, rather than running another figurative marathon and telling myself the lie that I would rest when this book was finished, I made a different choice.

I asked my wonderful editor, Andrew, for a two-month extension. He very kindly honoured my request and offered much-needed support and encouragement. In fact, he was so much kinder to me than I'd been to myself. And although initially my trauma narrative told me that I was 'not a real writer' because I needed to ask for an extension, my compassionate voice, now strengthened by the much-needed rest, told me I'd made the right choice.

Taking time to rest, asking for extensions and advocating for ourselves is not being irresponsible or lazy. It's being wise. After I asked for an extension and began to slow down, I was able to focus on my mental health enough to realise that I was a workaholic. Like many trauma survivors, I initially ran from my trauma by diving into work and overachievement until I couldn't run any more. With the war in Ukraine, the duct tape I placed over my emotional wounds long ago ripped open. The pain I hadn't previously faced nor processed came like a tidal wave and knocked me down to my knees.

And for the first time in my life, I realised how much I was relying on workaholism to keep me going. In seeing things more clearly now, I lost my old coping mechanism, but I found myself.

At the depth of my grief, I saw that we can't wait to live until we meet some self-imposed standard. Tomorrow isn't guaranteed.

Of course, I'm not suggesting that you spend all of your savings and stop working altogether. What I am suggesting, however, is that you do not wait to start living.

Perhaps you've told yourself that once you graduate from college you'll start seeing your friends more. Or maybe you bought into the idea that you have to look a certain way before you can start dating or that you have to pay off all your debt before you can take a single vacation.

And when we put such harsh and cruel expectations on ourselves, we get stuck in the 'never good enough' narrative. When that happens for too long, we might miss out on important opportunities and regret our choices.

In fact, some of the top regrets that people have at the end of their lives include:

- I wish I hadn't worked so hard
- I wish I had the courage to express my true feelings
- I wish I'd had the courage to live a life true to myself, not the life others expected of me
- I wish I had stayed in touch with my friends
- I wish that I had let myself be happier[1]

Most people tend to regret the steps they didn't even try more than the ones they tried, even if they didn't succeed.

Knowing this, if you were to start living now, what would you do?

Would you write a book, try acting, take singing lessons, reach out to an old friend, or start saving up for a trip you'd been wanting to take for a long time now?

Think about it. Try it out. See what's possible.

And have a magical adventure.

1 Ware (2012)

TAKE AWAYS

- Forming a connection with yourself involves learning about the function of your emotions – paying attention to see what your emotions are trying to tell you.
- Getting to know yourself also involves spending some time getting to know who you are beyond your labels – beyond the job that you hold or the roles that you play when interacting with others.
- Getting to know yourself can help you learn what your needs are and how to meet them.
- You can use several different exercises to learn how to meet your needs and get to know yourself, such as grounding, self-soothing, the Dog in the Park exercise, and three-minute Appointments with Grief.
- You can practise self-appreciation and seeking guidance from your hero to continue building a loving connection with yourself and your sense of self-compassion.
- You can map out how you allocate your time in a pie chart to see how you are spending your time now and to set up a plan of how you'd like to spend it in the future.
- You don't have to wait to be happy, you can meet your own needs now, and there is no shame in having needs.
- You deserve to have your needs met. You deserve to be treated with love and kindness and also to treat yourself with love and kindness.

PART 6:

Connection with Others

Chapter 45
Just Like ME

One of the reasons we feel lonely is that we feel like we're different from other people. Another reason is that we don't feel seen or heard by them, or worse, are devalued and abused by them. This can make it hard for us to trust others, which is why we focused on self-connection in the previous section.

The more we try to fit in with others, the more likely we are to lose sight of who we really are. By spending some time getting to know yourself, you might now have a better idea of the kind of people you'd like to connect with and how you want to be treated. Finding people who share your core values – people who see, hear and value the real you – can not only allow you to feel that you belong, but it can also enhance the person that you are.

For example, if you care about the environment and join groups and organisations that share your passion for the environment, you will all be able to learn from one another and make a larger impact together.

In order to help you, the first half of Part 6 will focus on how we can cultivate meaningful emotional connections with others. The second part will focus on self-advocacy when your needs are repeatedly not being met.

One of the biggest obstacles to finding a sense of belonging is when we focus on what makes us different. Focusing on our differences leads not only to loneliness, but also to dehuman-isation and, in extreme cases, violence. In a groundbreaking study, researcher Susan Fiske studied participants' reactions to images of other people presented to them while they were in an MRI. When participants viewed images of people they regarded as similar to them, the compassion and curiosity parts of their brains became more activated.

However, when they viewed images of people whom they regarded as different from them, the brain activation in their MRI scans was consistent with looking at something disgusting and inhuman, like vermin. This is especially alarming since it is precisely this level of dehumanisation that leads to prejudice, abuse and violence.

However, when participants were asked one humanising question, such as, 'What kind of food do you think that person likes to eat?' the participants' brain activity changed. Just one question was enough for participants to engage in perspec-tive-taking and show empathic activations in their brains.[1]

Considering how we are similar to another person creates connection, empathy and trust towards them. For example, when people dance or even just bob their heads to the same song at a concert, they are naturally more likely to feel friendly towards one another. This effect works when people are dancing to the same beat, but not when they are dancing to different beats.[2]

This is also why people who serve together in the military, play or cheer for the same sports team, sing together or follow the

1 Fiske (2009)
2 Behrends, et al. (2012)

same fandom have a stronger sense of connection to one another than to the members of 'outside groups'. When we are a part of the same group, a group with similar interests, or when we engage in similar or cooperative activities, our nervous systems sync.[3]

When we are bonding with others, our bodies release oxytocin, a self-soothing hormone, which is also associated with trust and empathy building.[4] This is why cooperative games and escape rooms are often helpful with the intent of increasing connection, trust and camaraderie between people.

Another way to practise building our sense of connection with others is the 'Just Like ME' practice. The 'Just Like ME' practice is one of the practices of the Compassion Cultivation Training (CCT). CCT was developed by Thupten Jinpa at the Stanford School of Medicine.[5] CCT is taught online and in person worldwide and I highly recommend this course to anyone interested in learning about compassion cultivation practices.

The 'Just Like ME' practice is brilliant because of its simplicity. We can practise it any time, anywhere. And this practice can be fully silent and reflective.

For the purpose of this practice, especially when you're trying it for the first time, please only choose to focus on someone you already like or someone you don't know very well. Don't focus on someone who's hurt you or someone who violates your boundaries in any way until you build up to it, so as not to overwhelm your nervous system.

3 Yang, et al. (2020)
4 Chu (2017); Xu & Roberts (2010)
5 Jazaieri, et al. (2013); Jinpa (2016)

To do the 'Just Like ME' practice, start by looking at someone, listening to someone's voice or simply thinking of them. Then, tell yourself, 'In many ways, that person is *just like me*,' and begin to list those ways. For example, notice a classmate, a co-worker or a neighbour you come across. Think about what makes you similar, for example, 'Just like me, this person cares about helping other people, and just like me, this person likes cats, and just like me, they like to watch the *Avengers* films.'

You can also add some guesses to your similarities to deepen this practice. For example, you might say, 'Perhaps, *just like me*, this person loves chocolate. And perhaps, *just like me*, they listen to the Beatles when they clean. And perhaps, *just like me*, they've had their heart broken. And perhaps, *just like me*, this person feels lonely and just wants to be seen, heard and valued.'

See if you can intentionally try this practice this week.

This practice can be fully private and fully silent if you'd like. Notice how you feel before and after this practice towards yourself and the other person. See if there is a gentleness that might develop over time towards yourself and others. (And it is perfectly okay if it doesn't.)

This exercise can reduce our feelings of loneliness by increasing our awareness of our universal interconnectedness. When we are able to focus on our similarities, rather than our differences, we might feel less alone in our experiences. And that is my wish for you – for you to know that you are not alone. You're never alone.

Chapter 46
Friends

When I was a teenager, I would come home from school, and then do my homework as quickly as I could so that I could stay up and watch the night-time reruns of my favourite show – *Friends*.

Aside from the *X-Men*, *Friends* was one of the most important fandoms for me during my teen years. Sure, it was funny, at least funny for the late 1990s. But it was more than that.

Seeing Monica, Chandler, Ross, Rachel, Joey and Phoebe's character interactions alleviated my own feelings of loneliness, at least while I was watching the show.

It wasn't until well into graduate school that I learned about the concept of parasocial relationships (PSRs). PSRs are a kind of a one-way relationship we might form with a fictional character or someone we don't know personally, such as a celebrity. In many cases, PSRs can be very helpful in that they can serve as social surrogates for us. Specifically, they can play a role of a surrogate friend, family member, support group or a romantic partner. This can be especially helpful when such relationships are either missing or invalidating in our lives. In particular, PSRs can help us reduce loneliness, understand trauma, find a sense of belonging and increase empathy towards others.[1]

1 Broom, et al. (2021); Derrick , et al. (2009); Gabriel, et al. (2017); Rain & Mar (2021)

For me, watching *Friends* helped me to realise that I valued the kind of friendships where people would readily offer emotional and physical presence for one another. I realised that I craved a sense of a chosen family and a place where I would feel welcomed and supported.

If this applies to you, think about your top fandoms from TV shows, books, movies, anime or tabletop role-playing games like Dungeons and Dragons, cosplays and/or video games.

If you could bring any aspects of your favourite fandom or community to your life, which aspects would be most meaningful to you? Which ones would make you feel like you belong or perhaps give you a sense of purpose or adventure?

What activities do you imagine sharing with your chosen group in this way, if you could? Which of your needs would be met in this way? How would you be supported and how would you support others in such a group?

Practising these thought exercises can help you to figure out what your needs are, so that you can seek them out. They are possible. They exist. You are not asking for too much. And if you have a specific idea about what kinds of friendships you are looking for, you deserve to have your needs met in that capacity.

Chapter 47
Chosen Family

'Can't you wear any other colours? You look like you're going to a funeral,' my mom said to sixteen-year-old me as I was getting ready for school.

'Black's a shade. *Obviously*. And there's more than one,' I muttered under my breath.

My mom rolled her eyes. 'But do you have to wear this *shade* every day?'

I'm pretty sure I glared at her in a dramatic teenage way and left for school without answering.

Going to an enormous, diverse and artsy high school in New York City had many advantages. First, it was easy to get lost and maintain both your anonymity and your individuality. Second, there was a club or a 'corner' (either a literal corner or a spot on the quad) for everyone.

There were language-based corners, such as a Greek corner, an Italian corner, a Chinese corner, an Arabic corner and a Russian corner. There was also a theatre corner and a marching band corner. There was a leadership corner, an athlete corner and an Army Reserve Officers Training Corps (ROTC) corner. And right on the corner of 85th Street, there was the goth corner.

Before I started hanging out in the goth corner, I always felt like I had to pretend to be 'okay' just to fit in. I would put on some make-up and a fake smile to hide the pain of depression and loneliness that I wore like a wedding band.

But in the goth corner, people openly shared their feelings. My classmates in the goth corner opened up about their struggles with depression, loneliness, break-ups, parental neglect, and with self-harm and thoughts of suicide. This sharing was never showy or dramatic but felt real and authentic. It was also a place where many students came out about their sexual orientation. It became a safe space because there was a mutual, if unspoken, agreement to not only allow our deeper inner truths, but to welcome them.

For the first time at that point, I felt that my emotions were not 'too much'. I felt like I was welcomed. Most of the time there, I felt like I belonged. The goth corner became a kind of home I didn't even realise I needed.

That's the difference then between our true friends and our *sometimes* friends. With our true friends, no masks are necessary. We can be ourselves, and instead of changing ourselves to fit in, we are loved and accepted for who we are.

In July 2022, the *New York Times* published an article about the many benefits of having a chosen family.[1] A chosen family is not one you might belong to by blood, adoption or marriage. Instead, it is a person or a group of people who have become 'like family' to you. These are the individuals that care about you and meet your needs for being seen, heard and valued. These are individuals you've elected to be your family of belonging.

1 Kirsch (2022)

Chosen families are especially vital when our own families live far away, are deceased or are no longer a part of our lives.

'Family don't end in blood' is a catchphrase often heard on the American TV show *Supernatural*. *Supernatural* features two brothers, Sam and Dean Winchester, who hunt monsters and save people. Having lost many people closest to them, Sam and Dean form chosen families with other monster hunters. This depiction of chosen families was so meaningful to the fans of the show that many joined the online *Supernatural* community, lovingly dubbed as #SPNFamily on social media.[2]

One way to find your chosen family is to look for people who hold similar views or values to you. Too often, we find 'friends of convenience' – people we befriended out of convenience because they were in our direct vicinity. Friends of convenience might include school friends, co-workers, neighbours or friends we make through other people.

In order to tease apart true friendships from friends of convenience, ask yourself, if you didn't see this person regularly, would you still go out of your way to be their friend? Do you feel connected to them on a deeper level or are you merely spending time with them because you've known them for a long time?

Friends of convenience can still be fun to hang out with, but they don't qualify to be your chosen family unless they make you feel safe enough to be open and vulnerable with them. And that's okay.

2 Zubernis (2017)

The thing that makes a chosen family *chosen* is that you *choose* who is a part of your family and who isn't. And when it comes to selecting the members of your chosen family, it's not about quantity, it's about quality.

So, think about the kinds of people you would want in your chosen family. How would you want them to treat you in order to make you feel seen, heard and valued? How would you be able to do the same for them?

Perhaps you might look for in-person or online groups that meet your needs. There are conventions dedicated to specific fandoms, including *Supernatural,* that create a safe space for many fans to also share their mental health experiences and support one another. There are also some apps that help people to find a friend match the way that dating apps do. And remember, if you are looking for a kind, supportive environment where you would feel emotionally safe, seen and valued, chances are that other people are too. And if a group you're looking for doesn't yet exist, you can build it yourself.

'You're one of the most inspirational people I've ever met,' I once told one of my clients, 'Rita'.

Her eyes welled up with tears. 'I am?'

I nodded. 'Absolutely.'

When the pandemic began, Rita found herself unable to see the people she would normally interact with in person. Due to the lockdowns and recovering from a painful injury, she understandably felt lonely.

One morning, while attending her virtual AA group, she greeted them, 'Hello, family,' with her warm and caring smile.

The following morning, she did it again, and then again. Over time, the other members of the AA group began using the same greeting as well, 'Hello, family.' The greeting undoubtedly created a safe space for many of the attendees who were looking for exactly the kind of family-like experience that this welcoming greeting provided.

Several years later, Rita, not wanting to spend the holidays by herself, decided to organise a holiday party. She invited her fellow AA members and anyone else who was feeling alone that season.

The result of it was more impactful than she could have ever realised. Nearly forty people showed up. They thanked her for hosting the event because most of them also longed for a sense of connection and community that her party created.

In putting together an event to honour her needs, Rita created a safe space for people to gather, to see one another, to have a heart-to-heart connection and to bond.

Oftentimes, when we consider our own needs and create actions in which we can meet them, we can impact other people as well. Creating a loving community or a sense of chosen family through a greeting or an event can help bring people with the same needs together. People who are looking for exactly what you are looking for as well. Rita's kindness and courage in taking these actions benefited her and the people she interacted with also.

And yes, she is one of the most inspirational people I've ever met.

Like Rita, you too might have already changed someone's

life with a simple greeting or an act of kindness. And like Rita, you too might be able to organize a social event or a group that meets not only your needs, but the needs of your community.

Take your time. Find yourself. Find those who help you feel like you belong. Because you do. You always have. You don't have to pretend any more.

Welcome home.

Chapter 48
Fear is Your Compass

For many years, when I was feeling lonely, I'd flip through the contact list on my phone. I'd scroll through the phone numbers of my closest friends, wondering who I could reach out to.

Eventually, I'd give up, too afraid that if I contacted any of them, I would be rejected. I used to take fear at its face value, believing that if I was too afraid to reach out to someone, then it must be an indication that I shouldn't.

After a decade of studying human connection, I realised that fear doesn't mean we aren't coping well. It means that we care. And the inverse of our greatest fears points to our greatest core values. This means that fear isn't meant to be taken at its face value. Rather, fear is a nudge from our moral compass to consider the most meaningful course of action.

Just as we've previously done with coping with imposter syndrome in Chapter 26, we are going to apply similar techniques to get to know your fear:

1. Write out your biggest fear, for example, 'I will get rejected.'
2. Look at the inverse of your fear as an indication of what matters most to you. For example, 'I care about connection and belonging.'

3.   Think of one small step you can take to honour that core value. For example, 'I might be anxious to do it but I'm going to ask my friend to hang out or catch up.'

Practising these steps can change our relationship with our fear and anxiety. Instead of it being something that causes a freeze response, it can be something we look to for a source of wisdom, in terms of what's dearest to our heart. This can allow us to take action.

Chances are that just like me, you might sometimes scroll through the contacts in your phone but decide not to reach out to your friends because you believe you would be burdening them. What you might not realise is that they could be feeling lonely too. And right at the moment that you are thinking about texting them, they might be looking at your contact in their phone and thinking of texting you. And then, they might put their phone away, thinking that you are probably too busy and don't want to hear from them.

In fact, most people underestimate the impact of sending a 'just because' text, such as, 'Hey, I was thinking of you just now. Hope you're doing well. Thank you for being in my life.' Research studies find that the recipients of such 'just because' texts value and appreciate them far more than the text senders might have realised.[1]

Over the past few years, I've put a similar idea into practice. Whenever I am struggling or feeling lonely, I remind myself

1 Liu, et al. (2022)

that, *just like me,* my friends are probably struggling too. So, I send a caring, 'just because' text to a number of people in my contact list. I always make sure to send several of these texts at once both because I want to support multiple people and also because I know that some of them will write back, and some won't. And that's okay.

On days I'm really struggling, I make a supportive post on my social media of what I would want to say to other people who are going through something similar to what I'm experiencing at that moment. For example, I might post something like this: *For anyone who needs to hear this today, know that you are loved. Know that you are not alone. Know that you are wonderful.*

For me, I find this kind of practice helpful in feeling more connected to others. And if you are open to it, see if you would be willing to try it as well. See if you'd be willing to reach out to others either by text or by posting something kind on social media at times when you are struggling, as well as when you're feeling well.

Imagine that someone you know is feeling lonely *just like you.* What would you be willing to say to them?

Imagine that many people also feel the way that you do (and they do) in this very moment. What kind of a supportive and encouraging message would you be willing to text or post to help others? Would you be willing to text or otherwise reach out to someone you know just to say that you were thinking of them and that you hope they're doing well?

Remember that every step you take makes a difference in other people's lives.

Thank you for all the wonderful ways you help others. You matter and your actions make a difference.

Chapter 49
The Magic Zone

When we've been isolating for a long time, reaching out to others can feel impossible. And so we might wait to feel 'better', wait till we feel 'ready', or until we no longer feel anxious.

But the thing is, emotions follow actions, not the other way around.

When we are struggling, it makes sense that we might want to take a day or two to process what we are going through. In this case, hiding out in our room is essentially like spending time in a *safety zone*, where things are safe and comfortable. Taking a day or two to feel our emotions about what transpired – be it a break-up, a falling-out or another painful experience – can give us the time that we need to start to process this experience and begin to heal some of our emotional wounds.

Safety/
Avoidance
Zone

Magic Zone

Overwhelm Zone

However, the problem arises when we spend too much time in our safety zone without stepping outside of it. If we start hiding out in our room (or another location) for too long, avoiding social interactions and meaningful activities, we are likely to feel much worse as a result.

You see, if we spend too much time in the safety zone, it starts turning into an avoidance zone. The problem with the avoidance zone is that it is exactly where depression lives, meaning that the more you try to avoid feeling depressed by staying inside your safety zone, the more depressed you are going to feel over time.

But the opposite is true also, meaning that if you push yourself too far outside of your safety zone, you are likely to feel really overwhlemed and feel depleted afterward.

So then, what is the solution?

The key is to regularly practise taking *small steps* outside of our safety zone. We can do this by imagining our safety zone as kind of a target that you might see at an archery practice.

At the very centre of the target is the bull's-eye – this is the *safety zone*. Remember that it's okay for us to spend 1–2 days at a time there but if we spend too much time exclusively in the safety zone, it turns into the avoidance zone, making us feel worse. We also don't want to rush all the way out of our safety zone and end up in the overwhelm zone.

But in-between the safety zone and the overwhelm zone is a place called *the magic zone*. Taking a small step outside of the safety zone allows us to step into the magic zone, where we can connect with other people and engage in meaningful activities without getting triggered and overwhelmed. Things you might do in the magic zone include being productive (such as cleaning or doing your laundry), connecting with good friends or being playful without pushing yourself beyond your limits.

The *overwhelm zone* is where we might land when we ignore our needs and feelings. This zone is also not helpful because it causes overstimulation and depletes us of our resources (our internal spoons) too quickly, making it less likely that we would be willing to step out of our safety zone anytime soon.

The hardest part of breaking a pattern of self-isolation is taking the first step, either a literal step outside of your door or a metaphorical step of confiding in a trusted friend, for example. But once we take that initial step, it might be easier to take additional steps. And remember that should you ever find yourself in the overwhelm zone, it is perfectly okay to take a step back to the safety zone again, recharge for a day or two, and then get back out to your magic zone.

If you're willing, please think about what each of these zones looks like for you. For example, my safety zone includes my room, where I can quietly read, spend time with my cats, recharge and reduce overstimulation. My magic zone includes going to a coffee shop or a bookstore with my partner or a few close friends. And my overwhelm zone includes large birthday parties, holiday parties, and crowded airports.

What do each of your zones look like?

Which steps would you be willing to take to charge up in your safety zone and then step out into your magic zone?

Try it out and remember that there's no rush and no

pressure. This is your journey. You're allowed to make it work for you. Go as slowly as you need to.

You've got this!

Chapter 50
Turning 'What–if' into 'If–then'

Having gone through the gut-wrenching experiences of embarrassment, bullying, or a shame spiral in the past, we often worry about it happening again. Of course, it's important to try our best, whether we're referring to our work, dating or interpersonal relationships. Yet sometimes, in an effort to avoid experiencing the pain of bullying or shame again, we might focus so much on being 'perfect' and 'not making mistakes', that we lose ourselves in the process.

We might be so afraid of falling into the shame spiral that we fall victim to all the terrifying *what-if* scenarios that our mind conjures up.

What if I make a mistake?

What if I get rejected?

What if I do something wrong or hurt someone's feelings?

Of course, all of these *what-ifs* point to your core values. Remember that the inverse of your greatest fears points to your greatest core values.

And so, of course you'd have these *what-if* concerns. You have them because you care!

But how do we manage them? How do we keep them from paralysing us into inaction?

Some people focus on examining the possibilities of these

outcomes. This would mean asking yourself, *What is the probability of this actually happening?* In many cases, our *what-if* thoughts have a very low chance of occurring in such an extreme way as we imagine.

This technique of analysing the probability of our *what-if*s coming true is helpful for some people but not others. For some of us, we might still hold on to the idea that our *what-if* could happen.

And they could. They are still possible, even if they are unlikely.

Hence, a method I like to use when I'm overwhelmed with the *what-if*s is turning those *what-if*s into *if-then*s. This technique works kind of like a fire drill. Of course we hope it doesn't happen at all, but if it does, we know exactly what to do.

For example, if you are considering reaching out to a friend for support, your *what-if* might be telling you, *What if my friend gets annoyed at me for reaching out?* or, *What if they're busy?* or, *What if they don't respond?*

After identifying your *what-if*s, we would rewrite them in *if-then* structure.

For example:

What-if thought: 'What if my friend is unavailable?'

If-then thought: 'If my friend is unavailable to support me, then I will reach out to someone else.'

What-if thought: 'What if my friend is annoyed with me for asking for support?'

If-then thought: 'If my friend is annoyed with me for reaching out for support, then I will understandably be hurt. I will process this event with another friend or with my therapist, or by myself. I will at a later time ask to talk to my friend about this, try to understand their perspective and share mine. If they are understanding and kind, then we can repair this rupture. If they are not, then I will need to consider whether or not they are a good friend. I deserve better than to be mistreated and invalidated, and if they are consistently not being a good friend, then I will need to rethink our friendship.'

Now, see if you can try it out yourself about a situation you are feeling nervous about:

What-if thought: ....

If-then thought: ....

....

What-if thought: ....

If-then thought: ....

....

What-if thought: ....

If-then thought: ....

....

As you can see, these exercises aren't easy. Going through them can be scary and painful at times but not addressing the issue will be scarier and a lot more painful.

Try them out and see if you find them helpful. Feel free to use them as you see fit.

Remember that you don't have to do this alone. I'm right here in your corner. I believe in you and we'll get through this together.

Chapter 51
Friendship Love Languages

When my dear friend Nigel passed away in March of 2021, I was devastated. And I was also surprised that several of my closest friends neither called nor texted to check on me.

At first, I took the time – four months – to focus on my grief. But at the end of the four months, I was still struggling with not understanding why my friends didn't call.

It took just about all the internal battery I had in me to contact them each individually to express how hurt I was that they didn't reach out.

The results surprised me and them. Each of my friends stated that they wanted to reach out but didn't think that it was appropriate. They realised how big a loss I was going through and were practising keeping a respectful distance to give me time to heal, especially because even though they knew Nigel and I were close, they weren't close to him themselves. That was when I realised that although we often hear about love languages in romantic relationships,[1] we don't usually talk about friendship love languages, even though they also exist, and are just as important to maintaining our platonic relationships as the romantic ones.

1 Chapman & Campbell (2008)

Briefly, the five identified love languages for romantic relationships are:

1. **Physical touch** – hugs, hand holding and cuddles. Interestingly, a twenty-second hug can lower cortisol (our stress hormone)[2] and elevate our self-soothing hormone, oxytocin.
2. **Acts of service** – preparing food for the other person, helping them move or cleaning their space.
3. **Quality time** – spending time together, listening to one another or sharing an activity together.
4. **Words of affirmation** – these could be statements such as 'I love you', 'I believe in you' and 'I value you'.
5. **Gifts** – these could be expensive gifts, but they can also be small tokens of love, such as a card or a letter, a new book or a paintbrush.[3]

As I was considering friendship love languages, I conducted numerous interviews to find out what most people were looking for in a best friend. Here are the seven qualities I recorded based on those interviews:

1. **Validation and emotional presence:** someone who listens without interruption or advice giving. They are present and validating, saying things such as, 'I see

2 Berretz, et al. (2022)
3 Chapman & Campbell (2008)

your pain. It makes sense you'd feel this way. I'm in your corner.' This is someone who would keep your secrets and be a trusted confidant and ally.

2. **Cheerleading:** someone who offers encouragement, such as attending your events, as if to say, 'You've got this! I believe in you.'

3. **Tokens of affection:** someone who shares fun memes, small gifts, texts, anything to say, 'I saw it and I thought of you.'

4. **Playfulness:** someone who you can be silly with; someone you can laugh with who will distract you or cheer you up as needed.

5. **Adventure:** an adventure friend is up for fun and geeking out together. They're willing to travel with you, go to a concert, sporting event or a comic convention.

6. **Calm and chill:** someone who understands when you need space and honours your boundaries. You can count on them to hang with you with no drama. You can catch up or watch TV, and it feels easy and laid back.

7. **Showing up:** someone willing to help you move, pick you up from the airport or help you cook. They will take you to doctor's appointments and reach out to check on you if they know you've been struggling.

It's important to think about which friendship love languages are most important to you and in which situations. It might be worthwhile to have a conversation about friend love languages with your friends.

Here are some questions to potentially consider:

- Which are your top two friendship love languages?
- What are your friends' top two love languages?
- How do you want to be supported when you are going through a hard time?
- How does your friend want to be supported when they are going through a hard time?

Conversations like these can help you avoid potential misunderstandings, give you a vocabulary to discuss your needs with your friends and, in the longer term, can strengthen your friendship.

Sometimes, the people closest to you will fail to meet your needs, not because they intend to, but because they don't fully understand what your needs are. It is perfectly okay to tell them. You deserve to be supported in the way that you need to. You are worth it.

Chapter 52

Connection Ruptures and Connection Repairs

'We've only been together for six months, but we fight several times per week. Is it normal for couples to fight this much?' one of my clients, 'Casey', asked me in one of our sessions.

I told Casey the same thing I've told many other clients: 'It's not about how many fights you have. It's about *how* you fight that matters.'

Ruptures happen. They happen even in the most loving relationships and in the best of friendships. A good relationship (romantic or otherwise) isn't about never having fights. It's about *how* you fight – it's about whether you communicate kindly, respectfully and effectively, even when you disagree.

Before we look at how to repair a connection rupture, let's examine why they happen in the first place.

The biggest ruptures happen when one or more people do not feel seen, heard, respected or valued.

Drs John and Julie Gottman identified four specific patterns of ruptures, which they call the Four Horsemen, because these can lead to a metaphoric apocalypse of a caring connection. The Four Horsemen of Relationships include *contempt* (communicating with sarcasm, ridicule and intentional disrespect), *criticism* (attacking the core of one's character), *stonewalling* (giving the silent treatment) and *defensiveness* (using excuses and lacking in accountability). The reason why these communication patterns cause ruptures in relationships is that they make the other person feel unheard, frustrated and lonely in the relationship.[1]

After reviewing these four communication patterns, Casey reported that when she fought with her partner, she was often critical, while her partner would get defensive and stonewall her. Having identified these patterns, Casey was able to have a conversation with her partner, in which the two agreed to respectfully point out to each other when they were engaging in these patterns. They agreed that when the other partner would indicate that one or more of these patterns would take place, they would pause, take a few minutes to breathe and reflect, and reset the goal of their conversation to hear each other as respectfully as possible. Although Casey reported that she and her partner still occasionally fought, she also reported that the frequency and the intensity of their arguments got a lot better.

Take some time to observe if any of these patterns are emerging in your relationships, romantic or otherwise, and take note of them. Just observe for now. Once we can observe it and name it, we can, over time, learn how to respond.

Connection Repairs

Nearly every rupture can be repaired if all involved parties are willing to work at it.

1 Earnshaw (2021)

And perhaps the biggest mistake people fall for is to give into *response urgency* – thinking that they have to resolve the conflict immediately, right now. Trying to resolve a conflict quickly, while one or more people are highly upset, will likely not resolve the rupture, it will worsen it.

The second big mistake people make is to storm out, hang up the phone, shut down or stop texting back without any communication. This is *emotional abandonment*. And although emotional abandonment might allow the person who stepped away to feel better, it will destabilise the other person and worsen the rupture.

Instead of engaging in either response urgency or emotional abandonment, a more skilful technique is what self-compassion teacher Michelle Becker calls a *self-compassion break*.

A self-compassion break is an intentional time-out from the conflict to reduce the response urgency and consider the most skilful way to listen to the other person and communicate your needs.

Rules of the self-compassion break:

- Anyone can request a self-compassion break at any time.
- In order to request a self-compassion break, it's important to state that you are requesting it and to specify its duration. For example, you can say, 'I need a self-compassion break. I'm going to go to another room for thirty minutes and after that, we will continue this conversation.'

- Specify not just *when* you'll be back but that *you will* continue the conversation.

- All parties need to honour the self-compassion break. That means that once it's called, all parties agree to honour each other's boundaries and wait to talk until the end of the self-compassion break. That means no calling or texting each other during the break.

- During the break, you can focus on your breathing or on writing out how you are feeling in order to process what you are going through. Think about what is most important for you to get across to the other person.

- Be punctual about returning from your break, so as not to rupture your trust with the other person. It can be helpful to set an alarm.

- Take turns communicating your needs and compassionately listening to the other person. When you are listening, don't interrupt. Just listen and try to understand. Try to use a warm tone and kind words if you are speaking.

- Take additional self-compassion breaks as you need or table the discussion to another day. There's no rush to resolve a big issue in one night. It's okay to take time.

- Even if your discussion isn't complete or you decided to table it for later, wrap up the day with kind and compassionate support or reassurance for one another, in order to provide emotional safety. For example, you can say, 'I know we are both upset and frustrated right now. Please know that I love you and appreciate you, and I'm confident we will resolve this together.'

Practising these steps can allow everyone involved to be as skilful as possible when attempting to resolve a conflict. The more we try to rush this process, the less skilful we are, and the less we are able to hear the other person. That's why it's important to go slow, take time, breathe and take one or multiple self-compassion breaks.

Before practising a self-compassion break for the first time, it's a good idea to introduce this concept by discussing it with the other person, ideally when things are calm. This way, when you practise it, it is not a surprise to the other person, and it is not quite as jarring as it can be if it's first brought up during an argument.

Self-compassion breaks also allow us to practise *compassion triage*, so that we can attend to our own needs first, and therefore be more present to the needs of others afterward.

When paramedics arrive at the scene of an accident, they assess the situation in order to figure out who will receive care first. For example, if one person is bleeding out and another has a broken leg, the paramedics will treat the person who is bleeding out first.

Everyone will receive care but the order in which care is received matters.

And sometimes in a conflict with a person we care about, or in a confrontation with a difficult person, the person who is 'bleeding out' the most is you. And that means that it is not only okay to practise a self-compassion break in conflicts, but it is also necessary.

And if you and a loved one are having an argument that hurt

you, it is okay for you to triage your needs. This might mean that you respectfully tell them that you need a few minutes to take a self-compassion break, so that you can take care of your needs before focusing on others.

Taking time to soothe and support yourself can give you the space and the resources to be more skilful in resolving the conflict you are facing.

Remember, fights happen. What matters isn't trying to avoid fights. What matters is *how* we fight. And if you and the people you care about can treat one another with kindness and compassion, you can mend even the biggest ruptures.

Chapter 53
Dealing with Unhealed People

We all have days when we are too overwhelmed, maxed out and burned out. When we are physically or emotionally depleted, we are less likely to be as kind and skilful as we would otherwise be.

That's okay, it happens to everyone. Whenever possible, we can apologise and learn from our mistakes.

Similarly, all people in our lives also have days when they are depleted and less skilful. And that's okay too.

However, there's a big difference between someone who occasionally has a bad day and a 'toxic' person. The word 'toxic' is thrown out a lot lately, so let's figure out what it actually means.

A person who is kind and considerate might need time to recover from a bad day, but then will be willing to hear you out, apologise and learn from their mistakes because they care about you and how you feel.

On the other hand, what is typically referred to as a 'toxic person' is one who consistently invalidates you, insults you and makes you feel devalued. Spending time with individuals who fall into this category will usually make you feel lonely, frustrated, unheard, confused and overwhelmed, as if you carefully have to choose everything you say and do around them.

There's a popular expression: 'Hurt people hurt people, but healed people heal people.' I think that people who act in a toxic manner are often unhealed people. Referring to others as 'unhealed' instead of 'toxic' can allow us to humanize the other person, as well as to better understand them and have compassion towards them without the need to 'fix' them.

The main differences between an unhealed person and someone who occasionally acts in an unskilful way is that an unhealed person is hardly ever willing to hear you out and continues to engage in hurtful behaviour without properly apologizing or changing their actions. A proper apology includes a validating statement, such as, *you're right*, or *I hear you*, as well as the apology itself, *I'm so sorry*, and a plan of action, such as *I will be more mindful of this in the future.* On the other hand, inadequate apologies are usually accompanied by minimal accountability and invalidation. An example of minimal accountability might include a brief apology, such as, *Sorry.* Or it might include an invalidating apology, such as, *Sorry you feel that way, but I don't agree.* Minimal accountability can also include excuses, such as, *Sorry, but I'm just stressed out right now,* and a failure to change one's behaviour.

Here are some examples of toxic behaviour that an unhealed person might engage in:

- Shaming or berating you.
- Blaming you for how they've treated you, for example, 'You knew how stressed out I was, what did you expect?'
- Punishing you by threatening to abandon you, hurt

you, or purposely ignoring you.

- Sharing your secrets while knowing that you didn't want them to be shared.
- Violating your boundaries or raging when you set them.
- Repeatedly criticising you, parts of you or things that are meaningful to you.
- Being envious of you and making you feel bad for your successes.
- Gaslighting you, lying to you or manipulating you.
- Expecting unquestionable loyalty without reciprocating it.
- Expecting preferential or special treatment without reciprocating it.
- Never admitting to being wrong.
- Regularly being unwilling to hear you or to try to understand you.

If someone in your life engages in most of these behaviours during most of your interactions together, you may be dealing with an unhealed person.

Keep in mind that many people engage in some of these behaviours, some of the time. This does not mean that they are toxic or unhealed. If they are willing to hear you out most of the time, it might mean that they are unskilful at times, but hopefully can continue to work on themselves.

Remember, too, that even the most narcissistic people in the world are capable of doing good things some of the time. And if you find yourself defending someone, such as, 'But you just don't know them like I do' or, 'Look at these nice things they've done' or, 'It's my fault, I should have realised how stressed out they are', these are potential red flags.

Remember that you can be understanding and loving while still holding the other person accountable for their behaviour. Having compassion is not the same thing as enabling someone. To have compassion is to notice the suffering of another person and to wish to ease their suffering. We can act with compassion when we hold someone's hand when they are crying or when they are in pain.

When we are enabling, we are not acting with compassion. We are acting out of wanting to alleviate *our* suffering from seeing another person's pain. As a result, we might offer alcohol to someone who is trying to quit drinking, or not let another person know the consequences of their behaviours. These enabling behaviours do not help the other person, they prolong their suffering.

Some of the most courageous and compassionate steps you can take are to recognise the suffering that someone's behaviour is causing to them and other people they are interacting with and hold them accountable for their actions.

Anyone can exhibit toxic behaviours, including people we work with, our friends and our family members. In the next two chapters, we are going to review several strategies for advocating for yourself and setting boundaries with others to be able to honour your needs.

Please remember that no matter what, you never have to put up with abuse. If you are continuously not getting the support and respect that you need and deserve, then you are not obligated to keep that person in your life.[1]

You deserve to be and to feel valued. You deserve to be treated with respect and dignity. You deserve to have your needs met.

1 To learn more about setting boundaries, check out Nedra Tawwab's amazing book, *Set Boundaries, Find Peace* and Kristin Neff's empowering book, *Fierce Self-Compassion*.

Chapter 54
Making Requests and Self-advocacy

When 'Morgan' showed up for her session in tears, she said that she and her boyfriend, 'Josh', got into a big fight on their second-year anniversary.

'He knows that I like flowers!' she said tearfully. 'I thought he would have gotten them. Or that he would have planned something. But he just asked me what I wanted to do on the day of our anniversary.'

'And how did that make you feel?' I asked.

'Angry! He put no thought into planning it.'

'It makes sense. I see that,' I said. 'And how did you interpret his actions?'

Morgan shrugged. 'How am I supposed to interpret that? Like I'm an afterthought. Like I don't matter.'

'Oof. That's so painful. I'm so sorry.'

She nodded.

'Did you tell Josh you wanted flowers and that you wanted him to plan something for you ahead of time?' I asked.

She glared at me. 'I shouldn't have to. He should know.'

'Why?' I asked her.

She grunted. 'Because it's what I would have done.'

'You're absolutely right,' I said, 'it's what you would have done. We get frustrated when we expect that other people should act as we would in a given situation. And you deserve to be seen and valued. You deserve to be treated in the way that makes you feel seen and loved. And it is perfectly reasonable for you to ask for exactly what you want.'

Morgan raised her eyebrow. 'But isn't it . . . pathetic? To ask your boyfriend to buy you flowers?'

I smiled. 'That seems to be the narrative we're taught – don't ask for what you want. We think it's "selfish", "pathetic" or "wrong", but it's this kind of communication that can help you be more seen in a relationship.'

Morgan bit her lip. 'I don't know.'

'If you've ever ordered food in a restaurant, do you ever have an issue with letting the waiter know which item you'd like to order, how you'd like it cooked and which sides or condiments you'd like?'

Morgan shrugged. 'I guess I sometimes feel shy when I'm ordering, but for the most part, no.'

'Right,' I said. 'You deserve to have your food prepared the way you like it. And you also deserve to be treated the way you'd like to be treated in your relationship. It might be uncomfortable to advocate for how you'd like to be treated, and it's also necessary. So, if you want flowers, ask for flowers.'

Morgan took a long, deep breath. 'Okay. I'll tell him.'

She came into our subsequent session with a smile.

'How did it go?' I asked.

'It was definitely uncomfortable. I told him that it would mean a lot to me to get flowers on all our anniversaries and that I would like him to plan out our anniversary celebration. Like a do-over.'

'How did he take it?' I asked.

Morgan sighed. 'He said he was embarrassed that he didn't get me flowers in the first place. He said that he didn't want to be a *cliché* and couldn't figure out what to do or what to get me. He said that it was a relief to know what I wanted, so that he didn't have to guess. He also asked if we could plan our anniversary activities together, as partners.'

'And how did that make you feel?' I asked.

She smiled. 'It made me feel seen. I was also a little surprised at how relieved I felt that I don't have to worry about my needs being met. I guess we can just talk about each other's needs and work it out together.'

We all have our own ways in which we want to be seen and valued. And you have every right to advocate for yourself in any and all of your relationships.

In some cases when you advocate for yourself, your needs will be met. In other cases, you might be met with defensiveness or pushback. In these cases, you might need to take a step back to take care of yourself and figure out what you would like to do next.

At times, other people can be both unskilful and invalidating, especially if they haven't faced the same experiences you have. And that means that you are the expert on your own experiences, not other people. Just because someone doesn't agree with you, it doesn't mean that you are wrong.

In addition, the people who have been through similar experiences to yours but are invalidating your feelings might be acting out of fear. They might be too scared to explore their own trauma and loneliness. They might be terrified to see that they are flawed. They might be too intimidated to face their pain.

They aren't ready. They aren't a warrior like you.

In order to protect you and your well-being, let's talk about some ways to get your needs met by the people in your life. One way to get your needs met is by advocating for yourself. The simplest way to do this is by directly asking for what you need.

It is perfectly okay to directly ask your partner, friend or a family member for exactly what you need. The clearer you can be in making this request, the better. For example, 'I want to share something that happened at work today. I'm not looking for advice. I just want to vent and after that, can you please just say something along the lines of, *Wow, that really sucks*, and give me a hug?'

Being this clear and direct might feel uncomfortable at first, but it is also the most assured way to get your needs met.

When you're upset, most people, out of a desire to be helpful, will assume that you want advice or that you want them to *fix* the situation for you. Simply hinting at what you need won't be clear enough and will just frustrate you and the other person. So, you might as well be direct and specific about your needs.

In her book *Dare to Lead*, Brené Brown says, 'Clear is kind, and unclear is unkind.'[1] In letting people who care about you know your needs, you're showing them kindness by giving them a chance to show up for you the way you need them to.

1 Brown (2018)

This might mean that you will need to be very specific about what you want, really spell it out, maybe even multiple times.

When it comes to other people, if there's something you want, it's okay to ask for it as clearly and as directly as possible.

Let's practise.

- When you're upset, how do you want to be supported?
- Which phrases and actions would make you feel heard?

Consider the answers to these questions when you are communicating with others. You can practise advocating for yourself by making specific requests about what you need when you need it.

It is also okay to take your time with these practices, especially if they are new to you. They are not easy, and they might never be easy. When we have frequently not had our needs met, especially when we have a history of trauma or engaging in the fawn response, advocating for ourselves will likely feel overwhelming and very challenging. Take your time.

You deserve to be supported in the way that works for you and it is okay for you to ask for what you want. You deserve to have your needs met and you deserve to feel heard and valued.

Chapter 55
Boundaries

If you were able to practise making requests from the previous chapter and were able to get your needs met, that's wonderful!

However, some people, even those closest to us, even the people we've known the longest, might sometimes be most resistant to giving us what we need. This doesn't necessarily mean that they don't care about us. It most likely means that they are stuck in their ways and struggle when it comes to changes. This is when we need to practise setting boundaries.

Contrary to popular belief, a boundary is not a confrontation or a measure of disrespect. A boundary is essentially a way of saying 'no'.

Setting a boundary is communicating to the other person, verbally or through an action, that you will not engage with them in a particular way. It is an action to reclaim your voice and your power.

For example, setting a boundary might mean telling your friends that you will not be going to bars with them because you've stopped drinking, or telling your parents that they can't come visit you without calling first. You can also set your boundary non-verbally. An example of a non-verbal boundary might include not picking up when someone calls you when you know they have been drinking, or not responding to a text message right away when you are feeling drained or overwhelmed.

The most important rule of boundary setting is that the other person does not have to agree with you about your boundary in order for you to set it. **It is not your job to convince the other person of your boundary.** It is only your job to set it and maintain it.

In her amazing book *Set Boundaries, Find Peace*, Nedra Tawwab states that when we first set a boundary, we will likely experience a pushback.[1] A pushback is when someone tries to argue with you after you've set your boundary.

Here's an example.

You've set your boundary with your friends: 'I've decided to take a break from alcohol, so I will not be drinking tonight.'

Here's what a pushback from your friends might look like: 'Aww, come on. Why? It's my birthday. Can't you just start next weekend instead?'

In this example, your friend is pushing back against your boundary, with a clear intention of getting you to change your mind. You have three choices here:

1. Give in to your friend
2. Try to convince your friend by explaining why you're not drinking with the hope that your friend understands
3. Continue enacting your boundary repeatedly and without a further explanation

1 Tawwab (2021)

If you give in after your friend pushed back against your boundary, you will likely continue to not feel heard by them. Alternatively, if you keep trying to explain (or over-explain, as I often used to do) about why you're setting a boundary to someone who frequently violates yours, they will argue with your reasons.

Let's see how this plays out.

You: 'I've decided to take a break from alcohol, so I will not be drinking tonight.'

Friend: 'Aww. Come on. Why?'

You: 'It's not been good for my physical and mental health. I get very anxious the next day and my stomach hurts for days after.'

Friend: 'Well, just one drink isn't going to hurt you. And we'll make sure we eat beforehand and drink plenty of water after.'

If you are struggling with boundary setting, you might find yourself weighing out your options here and wondering whether you should maintain your boundary or give in to your friend.

As a result, your response might come across as less firm and more ambivalent:

You: 'I don't know. I still want to try to not drink for a bit.'

Friend: 'But it's my birthday. C'mon don't be such a buzz killer. Just one, okay?'

You might find yourself feeling frustrated and embarrassed, feeling pushed around by your friend and perhaps wondering if your reason for setting your boundary is good enough. (It is.)

You might then offer another ambivalent response: 'I don't know.'

To which your friend might respond with another push: 'C'mon. okay?'

Here you might be feeling frustrated with your friend for pushing back on your boundary but also exhausted from arguing with them. As a result, you might give in because you don't feel like continuing the discussion.

You: (sigh) 'Okay.'

In this scenario when your friend asked you why you aren't going to be drinking, they didn't ask in order to try to understand you. They asked you to try to find ways to argue with you and to convince you to do what they want you to do.

Let's see what happens if you don't provide an explanation after a pushback.

You: 'I've decided to take a break from alcohol, so I will not be drinking tonight.'

Friend: 'Aww. Come on. Why?'

You: 'I'm taking a break from alcohol, so I won't be drinking.'

Friend: 'C'mon, don't be such a buzz kill. It's my birthday – just one drink?'

You: 'I'm taking a break from alcohol, so I won't be drinking.'

Friend: (sighs). 'Fine. Whatever. I'll see you tonight.'

Notice that in this example, your friend wasn't necessarily thrilled about your boundary, but they stopped pushing.

Boundary setting doesn't necessarily feel good, and sometimes it's pretty uncomfortable – but being unheard and invalidated is almost always worse. And so, if you're going to be uncomfortable either way, you might as well set a boundary and choose the discomfort that will also allow you to get your needs met.

Here are some areas where you might want to set boundaries:

- **Time:** How much time and energy you can allocate to others. An example of setting a time boundary might be letting a friend know that you aren't available to spend time with them for a few weeks or letting your relative know that you only have fifteen minutes to talk to them on the phone.
- **Information:** How much you choose to share with others. If your friends like to gossip, if your family members are highly critical of you or give you unhelpful advice, it makes sense to limit the amount of information you choose to share with them.
- **Financial:** Setting boundaries with how much money you loan or spend on others, particularly if they have not honoured your requests or boundaries in the past (for example, friends who borrow money but never pay it back).
- **Professional:** Setting a boundary as to how many professional services you offer for free and also setting a boundary as to how many hours you work and how many projects you take on at a given time.

Even if you don't feel ready to set boundaries yet, you can

practise writing them out on a piece of paper or stating them out loud by yourself.

Think about a possible conversation between you and someone you want to set a boundary with. Try using the example of boundary setting and repetition without going into too much of an explanation. Write out the entire scenario from beginning to the end. If you find yourself too overwhelmed about the potential *what-if*s, try turning them into *if-then*s (refer to Chapter 50 for more information).

Keep practising on paper or by role-playing with a trusted person until you're ready to try it out.

Remember, your boundaries matter. You deserve to be heard. You deserve to have your boundaries honoured and to be treated with respect and dignity.

Chapter 56
Tomatoes and Bat Signals

My friends and I have had many conversations about how difficult it is to reach out to someone when we are struggling.

Even as a psychologist with over a decade of experience, I find it difficult to find the words to ask for help when I need it.

And so, I thought that it would be helpful to have a single emoji that essentially means, 'I'm struggling right now and could really use your support.'

In the last few years, thousands of people began using the tomato emoji as a way of reaching out to others for support.

I brought this up to my friends, and suggested that we also use a single tomato emoji to signal needing emotional support.

'Like a Bat signal!' one of my friends said.

'Exactly, like a Bat signal,' I smiled.

Please consider talking to your friends about the tomato emoji, so that all of you know what it means and how you can support one another.

Of course, you don't have to use the tomato emoji. You and your friends might agree on using an apple, a banana, a pineapple, or any emoji that feels right to you. So long as you all know what it means, that's all that matters.

You deserve to receive the support you need when you need it. And this is one way you can reach out without having to find the right words to ask for help.

You are worth it.

Chapter 57
Letters You Send

In Chapter 48, we discussed the fact that we tend to underestimate the impact we make when we reach out to someone else *just because*.[1]

A wonderful way to increase that impact is through expression of gratitude. Gratitude expression practices can improve a sense of connection for all parties – those who offer gratitude and those who receive it.

Let's try it out.

If possible, try to think of someone who is still present in your life, who at one point has done something nice for you. If you pick someone who's no longer alive, that's okay too.

See if you can pick one to two specific events that meant a lot to you.

If you are willing, please write that person a letter of gratitude, a text, an email, or make a voice recording expressing your gratitude. Please add as many details as possible.

Then, if you are willing, send the letter, email, text or voice recording to that person. If that person is no longer alive or you are unable to send them the letter, please practise reading it to yourself and imagine reading it to them.

1 Liu, et al. (2022)

Try to do this exercise two to three times this week, sending statements of gratitude to different people. This practice can increase our feelings of connectedness with others, and can reduce our feelings of depression and loneliness.[2]

Remember, in doing this practice, you are helping others. You are making a difference. Thank you for being the amazing and wonderful person that you are.

2 Renshaw & Hindman (2017)

TAKE AWAYS

- Chances are that some people around you are *just like you*, in terms of having had similar struggles and similar needs as you, even if they don't always verbalise it. By seeing our similarities, we can potentially increase our sense of connectedness and reduce our feelings of loneliness.

- You deserve to have your needs met in relationships. Sometimes, the people closest to you will fail to meet your needs, not because they intend to, but because they don't fully understand what your needs are. It is perfectly okay to tell them. You deserve to be supported in the way that you need to. You are worth it.

- If a relationship is toxic, it's okay to set boundaries, pull away or end the relationship. You should never have to put up with being abused or mistreated. You deserve better. You deserve to have your needs met.

- You can repair ruptures in your relationships, practise compassion triage and learn about each other's love languages. Love languages do not only apply to romantic relationships; they also apply to friendships.

- You can figure out where you fit in. And if the people in your immediate circle fail to meet your needs, you might be able to find and develop a chosen family.

- You can practise gratitude letter writing to increase your sense of connectedness with others and to help other people feel seen and valued.

PART 7:
The Impact You Make

Chapter 58
Movie of Your Life

Picture this: ten years from now, a major film studio is making a film based on you and your life story. Perhaps this film is called *The Story of a Real-Life Superhero*.

This film is about your life, as you've lived it until now, and about the steps you have taken from now on and over the next ten years. It's about all the people you've inspired directly or indirectly. It's about the amazing impact you've made in other people's lives and continue to make going forward.

If you're willing, I'd like you to try thinking about and reflecting what this movie might be like.

Please take a few moments to read the questions below, and consider writing your answers on a separate sheet of paper, your electronic device or speaking them out loud (but if you can't, that's okay too):

1. What would you want this film to be about?
2. If after the screening of this film, an audience member was to tell you that your story or your message inspired them somehow, how would you ideally want to inspire them?
3. If you were starting to make this film right now, which steps would you start to take today to make this message a reality ten years from now?

Spend some time on question number three.

Which steps did you list? How would it feel to take one of those steps, however small?

What if you took one of those steps this week?

Being able to imagine your idealised life in ten years can actually motivate you to start taking steps towards making it a reality now.[1] By taking at least twenty to thirty seconds to imagine your ideal future as vividly as you can, you can essentially prepare your brain and your body for making it happen.

With this practice, you can start to engage in the kind of life you'd like to build for yourself over the next decade. And if the concept of the next ten years doesn't work for you, feel free to think in shorter or longer intervals, as you see fit.

The truth is that you have already made more of a difference than you realise. You make an impact every day, with everything that you do. With every choice that you make. Take a step. I believe in you. You are ready.

1 McGonigal (2022)

Chapter 59
Big Things, Small Steps

If you ever have to climb a figurative hill, such as when you have an enormous pile of laundry or loads of homework to do, then you know that it can sometimes seem impossible to complete this task in the moment.

However, we don't have to tackle everything at once. In fact, that would be unwise.

It's better to take one step at a time. Just one step.

And then the next.

And then the one after that. All the while remembering your *why*, as in: *Why am I doing this in the first place?*

For instance, if you'd like to write a book one day, your *why* might be *to help people* or *because I just know in my heart that I need to write this book.*

Keeping your *why* close to your heart either literally, by writing it out on a piece of paper and keeping it close by, or figuratively can help you to remember the big picture.

In the meantime, focus on just the first step. Only the first step.

Not the last step, such as, *how will I market my book when it comes out* or *will I have to quit my job when I sell this book?*

Focus on just the most immediate step. In this example, a possible first step might be to consider what you want this book to be about.

That's it. No other steps. Keep your *why* in mind but focus on just the next smallest step.

And then the next.

Big things, small steps. Big things, small steps.

Chapter 60
Letters You Receive

As we discussed in Part 6, expressing gratitude to someone through sending them a letter or a voice recording can make a meaningful impact in their life and in yours. And for that reason, I'd like to invite you to consider the following exercise, to reflect on the impact you make in other people's lives.

As before, you can either write it or record it. No need to send this one out. It's for you only.

Think of someone whom you helped at some point. Imagine that this person is writing you a heartfelt letter of gratitude about the wonderful impact you've made in their life. What would they say?

We tend to underestimate the effects of expressing our gratitude to others and also sometimes might be surprised at how we feel when we receive a statement of gratitude.[1] Practising receiving gratitude in this way can allow us to notice what we really long to hear and allow us to feel seen and valued.

Try it out.

Because the truth is that you make more of an impact than you realise.

1 Kumar & Epley (2018)

A Letter From Me to You

I don't know if anyone has ever told you this, so, I wanted to tell you just in case:

You are wonderful.

You are 100 per cent absolutely and completely wonderful.

Yep, that aspect of you is also wonderful.

And that one too.

I know that *just like me*, you've struggled to feel like you belong. I know you've struggled with deep, excruciating loneliness.

Me too.

And I know that, *just like me*, there were times in your life when you've lost hope.

I've been there too.

And I just wanted you to know that I'm so glad that you are here.

And I know that you are here for a reason. Here, on this planet.

You make more of an impact than you can ever fully realise.

Chances are that you've probably saved someone's life through your kindness. Someone you barely interacted with online, in the grocery store, or at the doctor's office. Someone you made feel seen and valued. Someone who probably stayed alive because of you.

And they might never think to tell you or know how to find you. And so, on their behalf, I just wanted you to know – you make an impact every day.

And from the bottom of my heart, thank you for being the amazing person that you are.

Thank you for being YOU. Thank you for being wonderful.

Warmly,

Janina Scarlet

Final Thoughts

Loneliness is one of the most misunderstood emotions because of most people's assumptions that it refers to being physically alone. However, as we discussed throughout the pages of this book, loneliness refers to *feeling* alone in our experiences, regardless of how many people are nearby. When we feel lonely, we might feel unseen (ignored, ghosted, excluded or disregarded), unheard (invalidated, gaslighted or oppressed) and undervalued (bullied, abused or singled out).

As a result of having had these excruciating experiences and not having had our needs met, we might engage in the fawn response (people-pleasing), and struggle to meet our own needs and advocate for ourselves. We might mask who we really are, how we feel or what we want. Or we might not even know who we are outside of our labels and prescribed social roles.

In order to ensure that our needs are met, we first need to determine what they are. This takes time and self-study. We can begin our journey of meeting our own needs by becoming curious about what our emotions are trying to tell us. We can process some of our past painful and traumatic experiences by practising daily three-minute appointments with grief, writing in a journal or practising grounding. We can work to honour our own boundaries and work to restore our energy through paying attention to our internal spoons and batteries and practising non-verbal time.

Once we are able to learn about our needs and begin meeting them, we can start evaluating our interactions with others. We can ask ourselves, *Do the people in my life regularly meet my needs? Do they try? If not, is it because they don't know what my needs are, because they don't know how to meet them, or is it because they are not right for me?*

We can practise self-advocacy and boundary setting and step away from situations when we need to. We can also practise gratitude towards ourselves as a form of self-care and offering gratitude towards others as a form of supporting them and increasing our sense of connectedness.

As you continue your life journey, feel free to return to any pages of this book any time you wish. Like a teddy bear or a loyal friend, this book will be here for you when you need it.

Please know that your need for love, respect and belonging is understandable. You are not asking for too much. You deserve to be seen, heard and valued. You do belong and you matter, more than you can ever possibly realise.

From the bottom of my heart, thank you so much for allowing me to be a part of this journey with you.

And if you would be open to it, I would like to invite you to please fill out the UCLA Loneliness Scale. You might remember filling it out at the beginning of this book. If or when you are willing to do it, it can be helpful to take a look at your scores again.

Please take a few minutes to select your responses to the statements below whenever you feel comfortable to do so.

Please use a separate piece of paper or an electronic device to record and count your answers.

UCLA Loneliness Scale (Version 3)[1]				
Directions: Indicate how often you feel the way described in each of the following statements. Circle one number for each.				
Statement	Never	Rarely	Some-times	Always
1. How often do you feel that you are 'in tune' with the people around you?*	1	2	3	4
2. How often do you feel that you lack companionship?	1	2	3	4
3. How often do you feel that there is no one you can turn to?	1	2	3	4
4. How often do you feel alone?	1	2	3	4
5. How often do you feel part of a group of friends?*	1	2	3	4
6. How often do you feel that you have a lot in common with the people around you?*	1	2	3	4
7. How often do you feel that you are no longer close to anyone?	1	2	3	4

1. Russell (1996). Scale is used with permission

8. How often do you feel that your interests and ideas are not shared by those around you?	1	2	3	4
9. How often do you feel out-going and friendly?*	1	2	3	4
10. How often do you feel close to people?*	1	2	3	4
11. How often do you feel left out?	1	2	3	4
12. How often do you feel that your relationships with others are not meaningful?	1	2	3	4
13. How often do you feel that no one really knows you well?	1	2	3	4
14. How often do you feel iso-lated from others?	1	2	3	4
15. How often do you feel that you can find companion-ship when you want it?*	1	2	3	4
16. How often do you feel that there are people who really understand you?*	1	2	3	4
17. How often do you feel shy?	1	2	3	4
18. How often do you feel that people are around you but not with you?	1	2	3	4

| 19. How often do you feel that there are people you can talk to?* | 1 | 2 | 3 | 4 |
| 20. How often do you feel that there are people you can turn to?* | 1 | 2 | 3 | 4 |

*Items for questions number 1, 5, 6, 9, 10, 15, 16, 19 and 20 should be reversed before scoring them, meaning that you should score 1 as 4, 2 as 3, 3 as 2 and 4 as 1.

NOTE: Your score is the sum of all items.

What did you notice? How does your score now compare to your score in the beginning of the book? Keep in mind that your score is not an indication of success or failure. It is an indication of unmet needs. Are there any statements that changed (in either direction) since the beginning of the book? Are there any that stayed the same? What are some of your remaining unmet needs and what are some possible situations (if any) that would ideally change in order for your needs to be met?

Regardless of the cause, your loneliness matters, your need for connection is valid, and you deserve to feel seen, heard and valued by yourself and the people you choose to have in your life.

When you are feeling lonely remember:

- Reach out to others
- There is someone out there who needs exactly what you have to offer

- You've helped others already and will continue to do so
- You have a gift to share
- You matter
- I see you
- I hear you
- I believe you
- I believe *in* you
- I value you

And if you need any additional support, please also check out the resources section at the end of this book. Thank you for reading. Thank you for being you. And thank you for being wonderful.

Resources

In the UK:

If you are having a mental health crisis:
  Call Samaritans 116 123 (completely free and confidential)
  Website: www.samaritans.org.uk

To find a mental health professional in your area:
  Check out www.bacp.co.uk/search/Therapists

For information on how to stop child abuse:
  Contact NSPCC
  Phone: 0800 1111 for Hotline to report child abuse
          (24-hour helpline)
  Or 0808 800 5000 for adults concerned about a child
          (24-hour helpline)
  Website: www.nspcc.org.uk

For reporting domestic violence:
  Contact Refuge
  Phone: 0808 2000 247 (24-hour helpline)
  Website: www.refuge.org.uk

For survivors of sexual assault:

    To find your local services phone: 0808 802 9999

        (daily, 12 to 2.30 p.m., 7 to 9.30 p.m.)

    Website: www.rapecrisis.org.uk

    Free 24-hour telephone support service: 0808 500 2222

    Phone: 0808 168 9111 (24-hour helpline)

    Website: www.victimsupport.org.uk

In the US:

If you are having a mental health crisis:

    Call 988 (available 24/7 free and confidential)

    Text: 'HOME' to 741-741 (available 24/7 free and confidential)

If you or a loved one experienced sexual assault:

    Call or message RAINN: 1(800) 656-4673

        (available 24/7 free and confidential)

    Website: www.rainn.org

For reporting domestic violence:

    Call 1(800) 799-7233

    Website: www.thehotline.org

For information on how to stop child abuse:

    Call 1(800) 422-4453

    Website: www.childhelp.org/hotline/

To find a mental health professional in your area:

    Type in your zip code on www.psychologytoday.com

References

Ahola, K., Väänänen, A., Koskinen, A., Kouvonen, A., & Shirom, A. (2010). Burnout as a Predictor of All-cause Mortality Among Industrial Employees: A 10-year prospective register-linkage study. *Journal of Psychosomatic Research*, 69(1), 51–7.

Aron, E. N. (2013). *The Highly Sensitive Person: How to thrive when the world overwhelms you.* Kensington Publishing Corp.

Banskota, S., Ghia, J. E., & Khan, W. I. (2019). Serotonin in the Gut: Blessing or a curse. *Biochimie*, 161, 56–64.

Behrends, A., Müller, S., & Dziobek, I. (2012). Moving In and Out of Synchrony: A concept for a new intervention fostering empathy through interactional movement and dance. *The Arts in Psychotherapy*, 39(2), 107–16.

Berretz, G., Cebula, C., Wortelmann, B. M., Papadopoulou, P., Wolf, O. T., Ocklenburg, S., Packheiser, J. (2022). Romantic Partner Embraces Reduce Cortisol Release after Acute Stress Induction in Women but not in Men. *PLoS One*, 17, e0266887.

Borawski, D., & Nowak, A. (2022). As Long as You Are Self-compassionate, You Will Never Walk Alone. The interplay between self-compassion and rejection sensitivity in predicting loneliness. *International Journal of Psychology*.

Broom, T. W., Chavez, R. S., & Wagner, D. D. (2021). Becoming the King in the North: Identification with fictional characters is associated with greater self–other neural overlap. *Social Cognitive and Affective Neuroscience*, 16(6), 541–51.

Brown, B. (2015). *Daring Greatly: How the courage to be vulnerable transforms the way we live, love, parent, and lead.* Penguin.

Brown, B. (2018). *Dare to Lead: Brave Work. Tough Conversations. Whole Hearts.* Random House.

Brown, B. (2021). *Atlas of the Heart: Mapping meaningful connection and the language of human experience.* Random House.

Cacioppo, J. T., Fowler, J. H., & Christakis, N. A. (2009). Alone in the Crowd: The structure and spread of loneliness in a large social network. *Journal of Personality and Social Psychology,* 97(6), 977.

Carter, C. S., Kenkel, W. M., MacLean, E. L., Wilson, S. R., Perkeybile, A. M., Yee, J. R., . . . & Kingsbury, M. A. (2020). Is Oxytocin 'Nature's Medicine'?. *Pharmacological Reviews,* 72(4), 829–61.

Chapman, G., & Campbell, R. (2008). *The Five Love Languages of Children.* Moody Publishers.

Chu, C. (2017). *Role of Oxytocin: Social Exclusion and Suicidal Behavior.* Electronic Theses, Treatises and Dissertations. Florida State University Libraries.

Clance, P. R., & Imes, S. A. (1978). The Imposter Phenomenon in High Achieving Women: Dynamics and therapeutic intervention. *Psychotherapy: Theory, Research & Practice,* 15(3), 241.

Coan, J. A., Schaefer, H. S., & Davidson, R. J. (2006). Lending a hand: Social regulation of the neural response to threat. *Psychological Science,* 17(12), 1032–9.

Coghlan, A. (2013). Healthy Living Can Turn our Cells' Clock Back. *Health,* 2935.

Crespi, B. J. (2016). Oxytocin, Testosterone, and Human Social Cognition. *Biological Reviews,* 91(2), 390–408.

Derrick, J. E., Gabriel, S., & Hugenberg, K. (2009). Social Surrogacy: How favored television programs provide the experience of belonging. *Journal of Experimental Social Psychology* 45, 352–62.

Devine, M. (2017). *It's Okay That You're Not Okay: Meeting Grief and Loss in a Culture That Doesn't Understand.* Sounds True.

DeWall, C. N., MacDonald, G., Webster, G. D., Masten, C. L., Baumeister, R. F., Powell, C., . . . & Eisenberger, N. I. (2010). Acetaminophen Reduces Social Pain: Behavioral and neural evidence. *Psychological Science*, 21(7), 931–7.

Earnshaw, E. (2021). *The Four Horsemen of the Apocalypse: Four relationship habits that predict divorce.* Mind Body Green Relationships. https://www.mindbodygreen.com/articles/four-horsemen-gottman-research

Eisenberger, N. I. (2012). The Pain of Social Disconnection: Examining the shared neural underpinnings of physical and social pain. *Nature Reviews Neuroscience*, 13(6), 421–34.

Eisenberger, N. I., Jarcho, J. M., Lieberman, M. D., & Naliboff, B. D. (2006). An Experimental Study of Shared Sensitivity to Physical Pain and Social Rejection. *Pain*, 126(1–3), 132–8.

Eluvathingal, T. J., Chugani, H. T., Behen, M. E., Juhász, C., Muzik, O., Maqbool, M., . . . & Makki, M. (2006). Abnormal Brain Connectivity in Children after Early Severe Socioemotional Deprivation: A diffusion tensor imaging study. *Pediatrics*, 117(6), 2093–100.

Epel, E. S. (2020). The Geroscience Agenda: Toxic stress, hormetic stress, and the rate of aging. *Ageing Research Reviews*, 63, 101167.

Epel, E. S., & Lithgow, G. J. (2014). Stress Biology and Aging Mechanisms: Toward understanding the deep connection between adaptation to stress and longevity. *Journals of Gerontology Series A: Biomedical Sciences and Medical Sciences*, 69(Suppl_1), S10–S16.

Fiske, S. T. (2009). From Dehumanization and Objectification to Rehumanization: Neuroimaging studies on the building blocks of empathy. *Annals of the New York Academy of Sciences*, 1167(1), 31–4.

Frankl, V. E. (1985). *Man's Search for Meaning.* Simon and Schuster.

Gabriel, S., Read, J. P., Young, A. F., Bachrach, R. L., & Troisi, J. D. (2017). Social Surrogate Use in those Exposed to Trauma: I get by with a little help from my (fictional) friends. *Journal of Social and Clinical Psychology*, 36(1), 41–63.

Germer, C. (2019, January 30). Shame and the Wish to Be Loved. Center for Mindful Self-Compassion. https://centerformsc.org/shame-and-the-wish-to-be-loved/

Hamby, S., Taylor, E., Mitchell, K., Jones, L., & Newlin, C. (2020). Poly-victimization, Trauma, and Resilience: Exploring strengths that promote thriving after adversity. *Journal of Trauma & Dissociation*, 21(3), 376–95.

Harlow, H. F. (1959). Love in Infant Monkeys. *Scientific American*, 200(6), 68–75.

Holt-Lunstad, J., Smith, T. B., Baker, M., Harris, T., & Stephenson, D. (2015). Loneliness and Social Isolation as Risk Factors for Mortality: A meta-analytic review. *Perspectives on Psychological Science*, 10(2), 227–37.

Jazaieri, H., Jinpa, G. T., McGonigal, K., Rosenberg, E. L., Finkelstein, J., Simon-Thomas, E., . . . & Goldin, P. R. (2013). Enhancing Compassion: A randomized controlled trial of a compassion cultivation training program. *Journal of Happiness Studies*, 14(4), 1113–26.

Jinpa, T. (2016). *A Fearless Heart: How the courage to be compassionate can transform our lives*. Avery.

Jones, J. C., & Barlow, D. H. (1990). The Etiology of Posttraumatic Stress Disorder. *Clinical Psychology Review*, 10(3), 299–328.

Kaveladze, B. T., Morris, R. R., Dimitrova-Gammeltoft, R. V., Goldenberg, A., Gross, J. J., Antin, J., . . . & Thomas-Hunt, M. C. (2022). Social Interactivity in Live Video Experiences Reduces Loneliness. *Frontiers in Digital Health*, 43.

Kirsch, M. (4 July 2022). Good morning. A chosen family can offer love and support that aren't defined by biological kinship. *New York Times*.

References

Kübler-Ross, E. (1973). *On Death and Dying*. Routledge.

Kumar, A., & Epley, N. (2018). Undervaluing Gratitude: Expressers misunderstand the consequences of showing appreciation. *Psychological Science*, 29(9), 1423–5.

Landry, J., Asokumar, A., Crump, C., Anisman, H., & Matheson, K. (2022). Early Life Adverse Experiences and Loneliness Among Young Adults: The mediating role of social processes. *Frontiers in Psychology*, 13.

Levine, P. A. (2010). *In an Unspoken Voice: How the body releases trauma and restores goodness*. North Atlantic Books.

Lin, W. H., & Chiao, C. (2020). Adverse Adolescence Experiences, Feeling Lonely Across Life Stages and Loneliness in Adulthood. *International Journal of Clinical and Health Psychology*, 20(3), 243–52.

Liu, P. J., Rim, S., Min, L., & Min, K. E. (2022). The Surprise of Reaching Out: Appreciated more than we think. *Journal of Personality and Social Psychology*. https://doi.org/10.1037/pspi0000402

Luigi, M., Dellazizzo, L., Giguère, C. É., Goulet, M. H., & Dumais, A. (2020). Shedding Light on 'The Hole': A systematic review and meta-analysis on adverse psychological effects and mortality following solitary confinement in correctional settings. *Frontiers in Psychiatry*, 11, 840.

Marshall, Lois S. Broken Heart Syndrome. *Journal of Radiology Nursing* 35, no. 2 (2016): 133–7.

Maslow, A. H. (1943). A Theory of Human Motivation. *Psychological Review*, 50(4), 370–96.

McGonigal, J. (2022). *Imaginable: How to See the Future Coming and Feel Ready for Anything—Even Things That Seem Impossible Today*. Spiegel & Grau.

McGonigal, K. (2016). *The Upside of Stress: Why stress is good for you, and how to get good at it*. Penguin.

Melamed, S., Shirom, A., Toker, S., Berliner, S., & Shapira,

315

I. (2006). Burnout and Risk of Cardiovascular Disease: Evidence, possible causal paths, and promising research directions. *Psychological Bulletin*, 132(3), 327.

Miserandino, C. (2003). *The Spoon Theory. But You Don't Look Sick.* Retrieved from https://butyoudontlooksick.com/articles/written-by-christine/the-spoon-theory

Murthy, V. H. (2020). *Together: Loneliness Health and What Happens When We Find Connection.* Harper Collins Publishers.

Murthy, V. H. (2022). The US Surgeon General's Framework for Workplace Mental Health & Well-Being. Retrieved from https://www.hhs.gov/surgeongeneral/priorities/workplace-well-being/index.html

Neff, K. (2011). *Self-compassion: The proven power of being kind to yourself.* Hachette UK.

Neff, K. (2021). *Fierce self-compassion: How women can harness kindness to speak up, claim their power, and thrive.* Penguin UK.

Neff, K., & Germer, C. (2018). *The Mindful Self-Compassion Workbook: A proven way to accept yourself, build inner strength, and thrive.* Guilford Publications.

Neff, K. D., & Pommier, E. (2013). The Relationship between Self-compassion and Other-focused Concern among College Undergraduates, Community Adults, and Practicing Meditators. *Self and identity*, 12(2), 160–76.

Orloff, J. (2017). *The Empath's Survival Guide: Life strategies for sensitive people.* Sounds True.

Platt, M., & Freyd, J. (2012). Trauma and Negative Underlying Assumptions in Feelings of Shame: An exploratory study. *Psychological Trauma: Theory, Research, Practice, and Policy*, 4(4), 370.

Rain, M., & Mar, R. A. (2021). Adult Attachment and Engagement with Fictional Characters. *Journal of Social and Personal Relationships*, 02654075211018513.

Reinhardt, V., & Rossell, M. (2001). Self-biting in Caged

Macaques: Cause, effect, and treatment. *Journal of Applied Animal Welfare Science*, 4(4), 285–94.

Reis, S., & Grenyer, B. F. (2002). Pathways to Anaclitic and Introjective Depression. *Psychology and Psychotherapy: Theory, Research and Practice*, 75(4), 445–59.

Renshaw, T. L., & Hindman, M. L. (2017). Expressing Gratitude Via Instant Communication Technology: A randomized controlled trial targeting college students' mental health. *Mental Health & Prevention*, 7, 37–44.

Russell, D. W. (1996). UCLA Loneliness Scale (Version 3): Reliability, validity, and factor structure. *Journal of Personality Assessment*, 66(1), 20–40.

Sakulku, J. & Alexander, J. (2011). The Imposter Phenomenon. *International Journal of Behavioral Science*, 6(1), 73–92.

Sirois, F. M. (2014). Procrastination and Stress: Exploring the role of self-compassion. *Self and Identity*, 13(2), 128–45.

Stoddard, J. A. (Sept 2023). *Imposter No More: The Power of Psychological Flexibility to Overcome Self Doubt and Imposter 'Syndrome' to Cultivate a Successful Career.* Grand Central Publishing: New York, NY.

Strand, N. H., Mariano, E. R., Goree, J. H., Narouze, S., Doshi, T. L., Freeman, J. A., & Pearson, A. C. (2021). Racism in Pain Medicine: We can and should do more. In *Mayo Clinic Proceedings* (Vol. 96, No. 6, pp. 1394–400). Elsevier.

Tate, N. (2018). Loneliness Rivals Obesity, Smoking as Health Risk. *WEBMD Health News*.

Tawwab, N. G. (2021). *Set Boundaries, Find Peace: A guide to reclaiming yourself.* Penguin.

Van der Kolk, B. (2014). *The Body Keeps the Score: Mind, brain and body in the transformation of trauma.* Penguin: UK.

Vermetten, E., & Jetly, R. (2018). A Critical Outlook on Combat-related PTSD: Review and case reports of guilt and shame as drivers for moral injury. *Military Behavioral Health*, 6(2), 156–64.

Waldinger, R. J., & Schulz, M. S. (2010). What's Love Got to Do with It? Social functioning, perceived health, and daily happiness in married octogenarians. *Psychology and aging*, 25(2), 422.

Waldinger, R. (2015, November). What Makes a Good Life. Lessons from the longest study on happiness. [Video]. TED Conferences. https://www.ted.com/talks/robert_waldinger_what_makes_a_good_life_lessons_from_the_longest_study_on_happiness

Walker, P. (2013). *Complex PTSD: From surviving to thriving.* Azure Coyote.

Ware, B. (2012). *The Top Five Regrets of the Dying: A life transformed by the dearly departing.* Hay House, Inc.

Whetten, K., Ostermann, J., Whetten, R., O'Donnell, K., & Thielman, N. (2011) Positive Outcomes for Orphans Research Team. More than the loss of a parent: potentially traumatic events among orphaned and abandoned children. *Journal of Traumatic Stress*, 24(2), 174–82.

Xu, J., & Roberts, R. E. (2010). The Power of Positive Emotions: It's a matter of life or death – Subjective well-being and longevity over 28 years in a general population. *Health Psychology*, 29(1), 9–19.

Yang, J., Zhang, H., Ni, J., De Dreu, C. K., & Ma, Y. (2020). Within-group Synchronization in the Prefrontal Cortex Associates with Intergroup Conflict. *Nature Neuroscience*, 23(6), 754–60.

Zubernis, L. (Ed.). (2017). *Family Don't End with Blood: Cast and Fans on How Supernatural Has Changed Lives.* BenBella Books.

Acknowledgements

This work would not have been possible without the constant support of my incredible partner, Dustin.

From the bottom of my heart, thank you, honey, for all the hugs and kisses, for always believing in me, and for bringing me coffee in the middle of the night to help me to keep writing.

This book would also not be possible without my amazing editor, Andrew McAleer, whose guidance and faith in me has allowed me to keep writing throughout the years. Andrew, thank you for believing in me when I could not believe in myself.

My deepest gratitude to the wonderful editors who worked on this book – Amanda Keats and Alison Tulett, thank you for all your amazing feedback and support.

A huge thank-you to my amazing book coach, Erin Michelle Gibes: thank you for all the fairy magic in helping me to find my voice. An enormous thank you to my kids, Hunter and Eddie, for giving me the chance to be your stepmom and for accepting me into your family. And a huge thank you to my Chosen Family – Sherry, Rich, Kiére, Happy, Travis, Paxton, Sasha and Shawn.

Thank you all for being wonderful.

Index

References to figures appear in *italic* type;
those in **bold** type refer to tables.

Index